PRAISE FOR THE APPLE AND THE STONE

"While readers who choose *The Apple and The Stone: 12 Proven Success Strategies Used by Steve Jobs and Goliath-Killer David* may think this book will be about business success, in fact, the topic is much broader than monetary success strategies. Under this vision and approach, obstacles become prospects for growth that promise the richness of not just singular success, but a wider-reaching approach to life…

The Apple and The Stone is outstanding in its approach and specific in its tips.

Libraries seeking achievement-oriented guides that go beyond imparting advice and admonitions to outline the nuts and bolts of a program designed to propel self-help readers onto better paths of living will find The Apple and The Stone's thought-provoking, actionable outline just the ticket for top recommendation to a wide range of patrons seeking change on different levels."

— **D. Donovan**, Senior Reviewer, Midwest Book Review

"Dawson…channeling Malcolm Gladwell in this business book…employs anecdotes from the lives of Apple co-founder Steve Jobs and King David to inspire readers to meet present-day challenges. The author emphasizes the ways in which both men, one recent and one in biblical antiquity, found hidden opportunities amid obstacles…

His own experiences drive home the book's key lessons—emphasizing the necessity of working decisively in pursuit of one's goals…

He also writes of his own two-decade long odyssey to first complete a bachelor's degree and then a doctorate, and he discusses how embracing one's passions as an entrepreneur or creator can help to drive out self-doubt, which he sees as a silent, persistent enemy of progress."

—**Kirkus Reviews**

THE APPLE
and
THE STONE

12 PROVEN SUCCESS STRATEGIES
*Used by **Steve Jobs** & **Goliath-Killer David***

HARTFORD G. DAWSON, PHD

ACKNOWLEDGEMENTS

To my Heavenly Father, Creator of all things, who makes the impossible possible by His mighty power: I give all gratitude, glory, honor, and praise to You! Your boundless love sustains me, and I am forever thankful.

To my beloved wife, Heatherlee: Your unwavering love and support have been my foundation. From the first spark of an idea to the final manuscript, your encouragement made this book a reality. I cherish and appreciate you more than words can express.

To my wonderful sons, David, Aaron, and Josh: You inspire me every day to be a better man, father, and leader. Your laughter, curiosity, and strength remind me of life's greatest blessings. Thank you for being my motivation.

To my late father, Hartford: Your wisdom, love, and example taught me what it means to be a husband and a father. I still miss you and strive daily to honor the legacy you left behind.

To my mother, Amy: Your unwavering faith, kindness, and belief in the power of education shaped the man I am today. From childhood lessons to guiding wisdom, your love has been a beacon. I am forever grateful.

To my sister, Heather: Your consistent love, prayers, and encouragement have been a pillar of strength for me. Thank you for always being there and supporting me with grace and warmth.

To my brother, Norman: Your resilience, hard work, and dedication as an exceptional father have been a constant source of inspiration. I am grateful for your example and the lessons I have learned from you.

To my extended family and friends, God works through you to guide and uplift me. I am truly thankful for your love, advice, and support, which have helped shape my journey.

To my creative team: graphic designer Steve Kuhn, editors Michael Tizzano, Lia Ottaviano, Lydia Asare, and marketer Rodney Hatfield, your expertise brought this book to life. Thank you for your dedication, skill, and commitment to excellence.

Their contributions strengthened this manuscript in ways I could not have achieved alone. Any remaining errors or oversights are entirely my own, as I made further revisions after their thoughtful edits.

A WORD TO YOU

This book is for dreamers, fighters, and those frustrated by life's relentless challenges.

When setbacks pile up and progress feels impossible, *The Apple and The Stone* is your reminder that perseverance still speaks louder than defeat. Self-doubt, daily pressure, and the weight of expectations can feel suffocating, but resilience has the power to transform that frustration into strength.

Within these pages, you'll encounter belief in action—through David's fearless stance and Steve Jobs's refusal to accept defeat. Their stories aren't just historical or inspirational, they're mirrors reflecting the battles you may be facing right now.

Let this book speak to your journey. Let it remind you: Your challenges may test you, but they will not break you. No matter how difficult the road ahead, your dreams are worth the fight, and victory is always within reach.

With heart and hope,
Hartford

CONTENTS

INTRODUCTION

Your current setback is not your final verdict; just ask Apple in 1997. Apple, now a trillion-dollar tech titan that *transforms* the technological world and enhances people's lives with the iPhone, Apple Watch, iMac, iPad, and other devices, was on its last breath in 1997. Bankruptcy loomed like a heavy, dark cloud threatening to blot out its existence. The company Steve Jobs cofounded was careening out of financial control and speeding down the slippery slope to embarrassment and failure, the slope of no return.[1]

Dell's CEO, Michael Dell, reportedly remarked then that if he were Apple's CEO, Steve Jobs, he would permanently lock Apple's doors and refund the shareholders' money.[2] Years later, Dell said his "answer was misconstrued."[3]

Microsoft's CEO, Bill Gates, was reportedly not a big fan of Steve Jobs during Apple's early days. Gates once said Jobs had an "intuitive

1. Adam Lashinsky, "When Steve Jobs Returned to Apple," Stanford Technology Ventures Program, May 23, 2012, https://stvp.stanford.edu/wp-content/uploads/sites/3/2024/09/when-steve-jobs-returned-to-apple-transcript.pdf.

2. Dormehl, Luke. 2024. *Today in Apple History: Michael Dell Says He'd Shut Down Apple.* Cult of Mac. October 6, 2024. Accessed June 12, 2025. https://www.cultofmac.com/news/today-apple-history-michael-dell-says-hed-shut-apple-refund-shareholders

3. Tsotsis, Alexia. 2011. *Michael Dell on His Infamous 'I'd Shut Down Apple' Quote: "My Answer Was Largely Misconstrued."* TechCrunch. October 18, 2011. Accessed June 12, 2025. TechCrunch.

sense for marketing" but lacked deep technical knowledge.[4] Nevertheless, Jobs, fueled by perseverance, passion, determination, unorthodox thinking, unparalleled action, and fearlessness, rescued Apple from the precipice of doom and accelerated it up the mountain of success. After being fired, Steve Jobs returned to Apple and orchestrated its recovery, transforming a $1.04 billion loss into a $309 million profit the following year.[5]

Apple now resides at the top of the technological mountain as its innovative wearable technology is worn on wrists and carried in hands worldwide.

Apple is now one of the world's most recognized and lucrative brands, primarily due to one man's actions. In April 2025, Apple was listed as the top technological company in the world, with a total market cap of $ 3.172 trillion.[6] Microsoft followed at number two, with a market cap of $ 2.929 trillion. Interestingly, Dell was not listed among the top ten tech companies in the article.

This book explores Steve Jobs's strategies and reveals secrets about how you can apply them to your everyday life, overcoming any barriers you encounter, those imposed by others, and those you impose on yourself. You possess unlimited greatness and endless possibilities within.

In *The Apple and The Stone*, I show you how Steve Jobs and Goliath-Killer David used the same twelve strategies to improve their lives and positively impact generations.

Three thousand years before Steve Jobs's mother delivered him

---

4. Bill Gates, interview with *60 Minutes*, May 12, 2013, *CNET*.

5. Nick Hobson, "25 Years Ago, Steve Jobs Saved Apple From Collapse," *Inc.com*, April 19, 2023, accessed June 12, 2025, Inc.com.

6. Forbes India, "Top 10 Largest Tech Companies in the World by Market Cap in 2025," *Forbes India*, April 30, 2025, accessed June 12, 2025, https://www.forbesindia.com/article/explainers/top-tech-companies-world-market-cap/95180/1

to the world, a Jewish couple birthed a son and named him David. However, before David was born, a mammoth, freak-of-nature, nine-foot-plus giant named Goliath violently roamed Gath and other communities with rage. Many who encountered him never survived to tell the tale of their demise.

On several occasions when David was a teenager, the giant injected bone-chilling fear into Army Captain Saul and his soldiers with his thunderous and explosive speech. This fear imprisoned their courage. They scampered like roaches across the wilderness floor, fleeing in great distress as the terrifying freak of nature verbally and physically threatened them.

Due to his massive strength and war skills, many men were ushered to untimely graves. No one with a brain perfectly apportioned into the forebrain, midbrain, and hindbrain would dare fight Goliath, except the boy, David.

Yet, despite being a unanimous underdog, David felled the great giant Goliath with a small stone and saved his countrymen from becoming slaves. How did he do it?

This book unearths David's secrets and shows how you can pull off unprecedented victories against the Goliaths you encounter along life's roadway.

Whether you're a homemaker, a professional, a CEO, a nine-to-five employee, a coach, a singer, a student, a college dropout, or were just released from prison, the path to living a fulfilled and victorious life is within your reach, despite the odds. We'll discuss the strategies for achieving a fulfilled and victorious life in *The Apple and The Stone*.

This is not a technological book, nor is it a religious book. Its foundation is squarely (or roundly, or triangularly) built upon these two tenacious men who accomplished extraordinary feats in their lifetime and changed generations for the better. One used a technological vehicle, the other, the faith train.

At first glance, writing about these two men in the same book may seem strange or unjustified. After all, they lived in very different times. One revolutionized the technology and music industries, among others, with his unconventional thinking and strong personality. The other, a young boy and a significant underdog, achieved one of history's most remarkable and shocking upsets. What did these men have in common?

I will draw references from David's amazing defeat of Goliath and Apple's unprecedented success under Steve Jobs's leadership. Please note, however, that I am not implying that Steve Jobs and the teenager David in the Bible shared similar religious beliefs or personalities. From my research, I highlight the common threads that wove their strategies and adventures in achieving incredible feats.

The Apple and The Stone is cemented with strategies to help you achieve incredible feats and leave a positive mark on your generation and future generations. Yes, you! If you have doubts, this book will help eliminate them.

Whether or not you are confident in your abilities, reading this book will solidify your confidence and strengthen your wings to soar higher.

Happy reading.

THE UPSIDE-DOWN OBSTACLE

View Obstacles as Opportunities

Sometimes life hits you in the head with a brick. Don't lose faith.
STEVE JOBS

Apple visionary Steve Jobs was deeply concerned. The company he cofounded was entangled in what appeared to be a trailer over-loaded with financial troubles. His beloved Apple Computer, which he and his friends started almost nine years earlier, was in dire straits. He desperately wanted to resolve the issues. However, despite his best efforts, the situation only deteriorated. The pulp of his beloved Apple was beginning to ooze through the cracks in its skin. It was fading. Declining revenues and internal disputes among Apple executives were darkening the color of his prized possession.

If something weren't done soon, his cherished Apple would be crushed. It would wither, die, and be buried alongside so many other unfortunate companies in the grave of insolvency.

However, being optimistic, Jobs believed he would find a solution. He would find a way to revive his precious fruit and thrive again. He would do it if there were a way to inject juice into his company. He could and would beautifully rain innovative life into his dream once again. He would align the financial stars to be in monetary harmony.

Yet, unbelievably, he was denied the opportunity then. In 1985, then-CEO John Scully and the board forced Steve Jobs out of Apple.[7] It should be noted that Jobs played a key role in Scully's hiring at Apple. Apple suddenly became a forbidden fruit for him. Its once-welcoming doors had transformed into obstacles. Walter Isaacson's biography of Steve Jobs provides deep insights into his leadership and personal life. Isaacson describes Jobs as devastated but determined, viewing the setback as not an end but a challenge to overcome.[8]

The CEO and board members' actions screamed that they had lost belief in Jobs's ability to significantly contribute to Apple, his company and vision. Jobs, who spent nine years of his life laboring to make Apple the greatest company on Earth, was banished from the garden. No longer was he allowed to nurture the fruit his vision bore. No longer was he allowed to add the waters of his creativity to what he had so carefully planted, cultivated, and loved.

He was disheartened. Sadness, hurt, and disappointment latched onto him like leeches and became his closest friends. It would take Steve Jobs several years before he publicly recounted his feelings when he was fired. At Stanford University's 2005 commencement, Jobs mentioned he felt like a failure when fired.[9] He used "rejected," "public failure," and "devastating" to describe his emotions when he was publicly fired from Apple. Nevertheless, he didn't cling to those feelings for long. Within a few months of being fired, his perspective

---

7. Corporate Governance Institute, "Why Did Apple Fire Steve Jobs in 1985?" *Corporate Governance Institute*, December 11, 2023, accessed June 13, 2025, Corporate Governance Institute.

8. Walter Isaacson, *Steve Jobs* (New York: Simon & Schuster, 2011), 205-218.

9. Stanford Report, "Steve Jobs' 2005 Stanford Commencement Address," *Stanford University*, June 12, 2005, accessed June 13, 2025, Stanford Report.

shifted; what once looked like obstacles and opposition now appeared as opportunities turned upside down. What had felt like failure and hurt revealed themselves as blessings in disguise. He faced a choice: dwell in self-pity or pursue paths that would have remained hidden had he not been let go. He chose to search for new opportunities.

In September 1985, Steve Jobs pursued his first opportunity: He began a new computer company called NeXT.[10] He faced his humiliating firing from Apple by creating this opportunity from the Apple obstacle. He then created another opportunity by investing in and acquiring a company he later named Pixar.[11] He did not know it then, but this move would create even more opportunities for him, add weight to his bank account, and bring joy to millions of children and adults worldwide.

According to Biographer Walter Isaacson, the Disney Corporation worked with Pixar and produced some popular animated movies, such as *Toy Story*.[12] When Steve Jobs took Pixar public on November 29, 1995, he became a billionaire.[13] At that time, Steve Jobs was still fired from Apple. How ironic. His decision to stop feeling sorry for himself directly and significantly made it possible to find excellent opportunities. Steve Jobs saw and seized opportunities in the face of obstacles and challenges. *You should as well.*

While Steve Jobs was away from Apple, the company faced increasing financial difficulties. Over the years, Apple struggled with declining

---

10. Jeffrey Powers, "September 12, 1985: Steve Jobs Leaves Apple to Start NeXT," *Day in Tech History*, September 12, 2018, accessed June 12, 2025, https://dayintechhistory.com/dith/september-12-1985-steve-jobs-leaves-apple-start-2/.

11. Isaacson, *Steve Jobs*, 238–249.

12. Isaacson, *Steve Jobs*, 284–292.

13. Luke Dormehl, "Pixar IPO Makes Steve Jobs a Billionaire: Today in Apple History," Cult of Mac, November 29, 2024, https://www.cultofmac.com/apple-history/pixar-ipo-makes-steve-jobs-billionaire.

innovation and leadership challenges, leading to mounting losses. By 1997, the company was in crisis, creating an opportunity for Jobs to return and steer Apple toward a historic turnaround.[14]

Jobs was rehired at Apple in 1997.[15] He was given a second chance to save his Apple, and he used his knowledge of seeing obstacles as opportunities to save the company. However, he did more than save Apple, he propelled it into becoming the most profitable and beloved tech company in history. At the brink of bankruptcy, Apple's survival hinged on Jobs's bold decision to pursue opportunity in the face of overwhelming obstacles.

STEVE JOBS TURNED OPPOSITION AND OBSTACLES WITH RIVAL BILL GATES AND MICROSOFT INTO $830 MILLION

In Steve Jobs's biography, Walter Isaacson writes about his contentious relationship with then-Microsoft CEO Bill Gates. In 1997, after more than ten years of litigation with Microsoft over several copyright infringements and patents, Jobs transformed the conflict into an opportunity. He reached out to Gates, offered a truce, and the future became history.

Microsoft invested almost $200 million in Apple as part of the truce. When Jobs announced the peaceful solution with Microsoft at the 1997 Macworld Expo and the opportunity it created for Apple, many die-hard Apple fans in the audience booed. But before long, their disapproval was heightened to cheers. Apple's stock catapulted to $26.31 per share and added $830 million in market capitalization

---

14. Isaacson, *Steve Jobs*, 307–312.

15. Jacob Suarez, "How Steve Jobs' 1997 Return to Apple Saved the Company," *SlashGear*, April 19, 2022, accessed June 13, 2025, SlashGear.

the very day Steve Jobs announced the pact with Microsoft.[16] On June 30, 2025, Apple was $205.17 per share.[17]

What if Jobs hadn't recognized and seized the opportunity hidden within the obstacles posed by Microsoft? If he hadn't looked objectively at his opposition without fear, would he have discovered the immense opportunity to partner with Microsoft? Had Steve Jobs failed to see the potential for an alliance with Microsoft and to take that chance, Apple as we know it today with all its innovative devices, might have ceased to exist.

Can you imagine living without your iPhone, Apple Watch, iPad, or iWhatever? Would your life be the same? Even if you've never owned a single Apple product, Steve Jobs's influence still touches your pocket and palm. Android phones, for instance, now mirror many of the design philosophies pioneered by Apple; sleek touchscreens, app ecosystems, gesture-based navigation, and even minimalist hardware design. The ripple effects of Jobs's vision reshaped the entire smartphone industry. Whether you're tapping on a Samsung, Pixel, or Motorola, you're still holding a sliver of Apple's legacy.[18]

Before the 1997 agreement with Microsoft, Apple was a dying organization. Many experts attribute Apple's survival and growth in the late 90s and early 2000s to the Apple-Microsoft pact.[19]

16. Alex Planes, "The Day Apple and Microsoft Traded Places," *The Motley Fool*, August 6, 2013, accessed June 30, 2025, https://www.fool.com/investing/general/2013/08/06/the-day-apple-and-microsoft-traded-places.aspx

17. Yahoo Finance, "Apple Inc. (AAPL) Stock Historical Prices & Data," *Yahoo Finance*, accessed June 30, 2025, https://finance.yahoo.com/quote/AAPL/history.

18. Tim Bajarin, "Why Steve Jobs Went 'Thermonuclear' Over Android," *PCMag*, December 1, 2014, accessed June 30, 2025, https://www.pcmag.com/opinions/why-steve-jobs-went-thermonuclear-over-android

19. Stephen Silver, "August 6, 1997—The Day Apple and Microsoft Made Peace," *AppleInsider*, August 6, 2018, https://appleinsider.com/articles/18/08/06/august-6-1997----the-day-apple-and-microsoft-made-peace.

Are you prepared to sift through the rubble of your disappointments and challenges to uncover your opportunities?

When you and I find the hidden opportunities in our obstacles, it will be life-changing, even generation-changing. Like Steve Jobs, Goliath-killer David saw an opportunity when everyone else saw an obstacle.

DAVID THE TEENAGER

David is a young Jewish shepherd boy whose main responsibility is caring for his father's sheep. He has seven older brothers, three of whom are Israelite soldiers. David is too young to serve in the army and only visits the war zone to carry food for his brothers, see how they are doing, and update their father. This brought David face-to-face with Goliath on the fateful day, the day the unthinkable happened. The day teenager David took explosive, decisive action, he changed his life, his family's, and countless others, leaving a generational impact. This is like the day in 2007 when Steve Jobs launched the iPhone, changing people's lives and affecting countless generations. For now, let's get back to David visiting his brothers in the war zone.

The Israelite commander-in-chief, Saul, led the Israelite army and held the final authority over the war. He was also the king of Israel. In biblical times, just as now, nations often waged war against one another. Israel and the Philistines were frequently in conflict, particularly in Gaza. Interestingly, this is the same Gaza where Israel and the Palestinians are still engaged in battle today. The main difference between wars then and now lies in the weaponry used. The earliest weapons included spears, shields, sticks, and stones, not the weapons of mass destruction we have today, such as assault rifles, IEDs, bombs, drones, and fighter jets.

In the olden days, countries feared each other because of their fighters, not their weaponry. One fearsome Philistine soldier was named Goliath. He was the crowned champion of the Philistine army. He was the best of the very best the Philistine army could showcase. His reputation preceded him, and seeing him generated fear in all his opponents. He was a nine-foot-plus giant who handled the untimely placement of many men's broken bodies beneath the earth's surface.

Goliath was no joke. If he were around today, one might need to summon the Shayetet 13 (S13) to silence him forever. Goliath was a terrorist. He was a one-man killing machine, and he downloaded a ravaging fear virus into Saul and his soldiers' operating system. Goliath was whom Saul and the Israelite army faced at Sokoh in Judah. It is important to note that Goliath and the Philistines challenged the Israelites on their land, Judah.

Do not permit the Goliaths in life to become obstacle-residents in your space.

SAUL AND HIS ARMY SEE GOLIATH AS AN OBSTACLE

According to the biblical book of 1 Samuel 17, the giant Goliath had threatened the Israelite army for forty days and forty nights. The giant was so fearsome that when Saul, the commander of Israel's army, and his troops saw him, they scattered in terror, fleeing for their lives. Even now, gazing at the giant makes them forget they are soldiers. Saul and his men are painfully aware of Goliath's reputation.

They know he is a killing machine. They understand Goliath was once a child soldier who had killed before reaching puberty. Goliath had taken down men with beards before hair had grown on his chin. Saul knows this and is overwhelmingly fearful of the giant.

The army commander, the king of Israel, panics, and his soldiers follow suit. It's an understandable reaction. Picture a pilot panicking mid-flight: once the crew and passengers hear the fear in the pilot's voice over the speakers, anxiety ripples through the cabin. Fear, when modeled by a leader, spreads fast.

Despite being trained soldiers, Saul and his men find themselves devoid of courage in the face of Goliath's reputation and imposing presence. But then, the teenager David enters the scene, and chaos ensues. The future is never the same as the past. Saul fears his future while David brightens his own.

DAVID SEES GOLIATH AS AN OPPORTUNITY

David is not qualified to be an Israelite soldier and fight in the war, so he lacks firsthand knowledge of Goliath, until his father gives him roasted grain, ten loaves of bread, and ten cheeses to bring to his brothers and their commander, Saul.[20] As David approaches the camp, he sees fear and hears the soldiers complaining about the fearsome and massively built Goliath. David notices the soldiers, the men trained and responsible for protecting Israel and its people, in frightful shock. He does not understand why they are so afraid. Yes, the giant is enormous, but they are also trained warriors.

Though David is not a trained soldier, the very first time he sees Goliath and hears him speak, he is unfazed by the giant's thunderous bass voice and 125-pound armor. David is fearless, not because he's reckless, but because he's been tested. As a young shepherd, he's had to ward off lions and bears to protect his father's sheep. He may be a teenager, but he has already faced serious threats and developed the skill and resolve needed to defend what matters.

---

20. *KJV*, 1 Samuel 17:18.

Likewise, as you're reading this, you've already survived battles of your own. The proof? You're still here. And if you've made it this far, don't let today's giant steal your fight. Face it with courage, just like David, because your past victories have prepared you for this very moment.

David's first words reveal his fearless mindset. Instead of seeing Goliath as an obstacle, he views him as an opportunity and asks about the reward for the one who defeats the giant.[21]

Obstacles aren't roadblocks, they're launchpads to greatness. Find the hidden opportunities within them and fuel your breakthrough.

Obstacles aren't roadblocks, they're launchpads to greatness. Find the hidden opportunities within them and fuel your breakthrough. When you recognize adversity as a doorway to growth and success, you unlock possibilities beyond imagination. David, the young, non-military, unassuming boy, physically sees the giant just as Saul and the army have, and hears Goliath's threats. However, David is not fearful because he sees Goliath as an opportunity, not an obstacle.

David assures the army that they do not need to succumb to fear or despair because he is willing to face the giant himself. The soldiers are shocked. *Did they really hear what the boy said?*

They, the experienced men of war with resumes highlighting the brilliant victories of the Israelite army, are afraid of this giant, their nemesis, their obstacle. Yet, the non-soldier, too young to even fight in the war, courageously accepts the dangerous giant's challenge. What?

---

21. *KJV*, 1 Samuel 17:26.

Why? Goliath was infamous. The nine-foot freak was a sadistic killer. He had been the reigning Philistine champion for decades.

The youngster must be joking about his desire to fight Goliath. Yet, as they look at him, they see excitement and courage reflected in his gaze. To David, Goliath clearly represents an opportunity and someone worth confronting.

How do you view your current obstacles? Do you see them as opportunities? If not, how are you looking at them? No doubt, disruptions in any path or a breakaway in a highway that looks like an obstacle can be disheartening. Aren't they really opportunities to conceptualize, design, and construct a bridge? Aren't failed business ventures, broken dreams, and disappointments really the birth pains of new opportunities to launch new business ventures and birth bigger dreams?

There are opportunities in every obstacle. Regardless of how difficult or stressful a situation appears, opportunities for mental growth, intellectual development, technological advances, personal advancement, and other successes are present within the fabric of those challenges.

The problem is that these opportunities are not easily recognized. For instance, before the invention of boats, the vast waters of the oceans were merely seen as obstacles for those who wished to travel to distant lands. Today, the cruise and cargo ship industries have become billion-dollar enterprises.

My wife and I visited the Panama Canal in Central America in 2025. We learned it was only built because someone saw the land barrier between the Pacific and Atlantic Oceans as an opportunity, one that could save cargo companies five to six weeks and tens of millions of dollars per trip.[22]

---

22. Amaan Gulacha, "The Panama Canal's Role in Strategic Supply Chain Planning," *Forbes*, June 13, 2025, accessed June 13, 2025, Forbes.

Someone recognized the opportunity within the challenges of non-solid water, whale sharks, lion's mane jellyfish, and giant squids. They viewed the sea as an opportunity, not an obstacle. Someone perceived the waters as a pathway rather than merely a place for the sea residents who comfortably exhale and inhale while submerged. This opportunity has created jobs for many and allowed people to party and even sleep on the water. By identifying the opportunity hidden within the challenge, numerous individuals became millionaires and even billionaires.

STEPS TO SEEING OBSTACLES AS OPPORTUNITIES

The first step in viewing obstacles as opportunities is not to be intimidated. Fear can be a healthy emotion; however, if left unchecked, it will cloud your judgment, dampen your outlook, and muddy your perception. Fear can rob you of potential success. In fact, uncontrolled fear can cripple you.

As a young child, I stuttered badly, which made me afraid to speak in public. In Grade 2, when my teacher asked me to say my name on the first day of school, fear gripped my tongue and sealed my lips. I was unable to utter a word. It worsened when another peer loudly declared, *"He doesn't know his name."* Immediately, as if on cue, all one billion children, except me, of course, joined their voices in laughterous melody until Mrs. Hall mercifully ended the concert. For the record, *"laughterous"* is not yet recognized as an authorized English word.

It took me about 12 years after that horrifying encounter to rise above the obstacle of stuttering and comfortably speak in a group setting. Even now, decades later, I slightly stutter at times. Nevertheless, this obstacle has made me sympathetic to and extremely patient with disabled and bullied children, particularly those who have a speech impediment or learning disability.

It took me decades to realize that I could only overcome the challenge of public speaking by seizing opportunities to speak in front of others. Opportunity begins when you step into discomfort. The fear you have is the opportunity that can transform you. Therefore, I actively seek opportunities to speak at conferences. This book is a byproduct of my preparation for presenting at a conference in Africa.

Years ago, when my youngest son, Josh, was a high school senior, he asked me to proofread his essay about a childhood experience. After reading it, I realized he had learned to overcome obstacles early on, which has helped him a lot. He allowed me to share his essay with you. Here it is:

THAT TIME IN THE OLD YARD
(Josh Dawson)

My father often reminds me of "that time in the old yard" whenever I am faced with some type of challenge or adversity. The lesson I learned back then always propels me to run through barriers and never quit. I know now how that time in the old yard has shaped me, but not back then. It developed my character in a significant way.

When I was about six, I would always play outside with my father at the house where I grew up, the old yard. Much like any father and son, we would play catch and run around. When we used to play catch, I would get very frustrated with myself because of issues with throwing the ball accurately. I would see my brother throw the ball straight to my father, but no matter how hard I tried, I couldn't manage to throw the ball straight. It would always go off somewhere, but never in the direction I intended. The distance was not the problem, but rather the accuracy of the throw. This frustrated me greatly. My father would always calm me down and have me refocus on the task at hand. Although it was not easy, and it took a very long time, I was finally able to deliver the ball straight to my father.

This might seem like a typical experience that most go through. However, it has stuck with me to this day. That single experience has helped shape my character in ways I never thought possible. It has helped me create a strong work ethic. I failed constantly and would get frustrated, but I eventually persevered, because of the time in the old yard. Now, when faced with any challenge, I know that despite my frustrations, I will persevere. It is in my character to have the reassurance that I will always succeed in any endeavor. I just need to refocus and work hard.

Similarly, that experience has developed a boldness in me to always focus on myself rather than what others are doing. I would always watch how my brother would throw the ball so accurately and effortlessly to my father. It was one of the reasons I would get so frustrated. I used to wonder: if it could come to him so easily, why couldn't it come to me that way? I would come to learn that he, too, would have similar struggles in activities and that it just wasn't my time yet. Focusing on myself has enabled me to avoid getting caught up with distractions but rather focus on my personal success.

The distinctive traits that make me the individual I am today have been formed from the accumulation of many people, events, and experiences. However, the single experience of "that time in the old yard" has shaped many of these traits by itself.

Whether you are a CEO or a student, unemployed or employed, a person recognized by many or known by a few, do not let obstacles intimidate you. Do not permit fear to clip the wings of your dreams. You have the power to soar, to plant the seeds of change, and to cultivate a future that generations will harvest.

If success, well-being, and advancement are ingredients in your future plans, make a conscious decision now to revoke unhealthy fears.

Do not permit fear to clip the wings of your dreams. You have the power to soar, to plant the seeds of change, and to cultivate a future that generations will harvest.

Fear of failure has robbed many of their dreams. Would you still write a book if you feared it would not be good enough and no one would buy it? Best-selling author Kathryn Stockett told *Time Magazine* in 2009 that when she began writing her first book, *The Help,* she doubted anyone would read it, yet she kept on writing.[23]

When *The Help* was finished, she faced a gauntlet of rejection.

---

23. Claire Suddath, "Kathryn Stockett, Author of *The Help*," *Time Magazine*, November 11, 2009, accessed June 13, 2025, Time.

Sixty literary agents turned her down, one after another. Nevertheless, she refused to bow to fear or let it sabotage her calling. Instead, she leaned into the silence, sharpened her resolve, and submitted her manuscript again.[24]

Her defiance of doubt bore fruit: *The Help* became a publishing phenomenon, selling more than 3 million copies, remaining on *The New York Times* bestseller list for over two years, and reaching readers in 35 countries. The 2011 film adaptation soared, grossing $160 million within three months.[25]

What if Ms. Stockett had succumbed to her fear of failure? Please do not hide under the fear-of-failure umbrella! If you do, you will never enjoy the warm sun of success or the raindrops of triumph.

While there's no promise your venture will succeed like The Help, remember it's worth trying. You owe it to yourself, your family, and even future generations to open your umbrella of courage, and let the wind of perseverance lift it high. Ms. Stockett thought she might have struck out, but she hit a grand slam because she kept swinging.

Do not let the fear of failure stop you from swinging. It certainly did not stop Steve Jobs, who became the mastermind of one of the world's most profitable companies and a globally known brand.

STEVE JOBS ON WHY THERE IS NO NEED TO FEAR FAILURE

At Stanford, when Steve Jobs recounted the pain he felt after being fired from Apple, he referred to the certainty of death. This initially surprised me since his primary audience was young college graduates.

---

24. Susan Gabriel, "Kathryn Stockett: *The Help* Turned Down 60 Times," *Susan Gabriel: Southern Novelist*, August 11, 2011, https://www.susangabriel.com/writers-and-writing/kathryn-stockett

25. Suzanne W. Jones, "The Divided Reception of *The Help*," *JSTOR*, 2009, accessed June 13, 2025, JSTOR.

Yet, Jobs mentioned this certainty and beautifully contrasted it with the fear of embarrassment and failure. He suggested that fearing embarrassment and failure is merely a trap that makes people believe they have something to lose. He concluded, *"There is no reason for you NOT to follow your heart* (dreams)."[26]

Based on Apple's constant achievements and spectacular innovations over several decades, we realize Steve Jobs knew what he was saying to be true. There is no need to fear failure and no plausible reason not to follow your dreams. Deep down, I believe you know this to be true as well. Whatever excuses you throw at yourself for not following your hopes and dreams can be easily caught and discarded into the incinerator of your mind.

Go ahead; you can do it. You need to do it and do it quickly.

Based on information from his Stanford speech, these are some excuses Jobs could have used not to follow his dreams:

- He was given up by his parents at birth for adoption.

- He was a college dropout.

- He was homeless.

- He sold Coke bottles to get money for food.

- He walked several miles on Sunday nights to get a meal.

Certainly, generations are grateful that Mr. Jobs did not use excuses to kill his dreams. You will forever be thankful that you decided to follow your dreams. I am forever grateful that I did not give up on myself.

It has been several years since I considered writing a book. In fact,

26. Steve Jobs, "Stanford Commencement Address," *Stanford University*, June 12, 2005, accessed June 13, 2025, Stanford.

my wife and sister have been encouraging me to do so for years. But the excuses for writing the book always multiplied. I had to make a concerted mental effort to begin writing this book.

One of the triggers that inspired me to start writing was reading Nikkie Pryce's book *Dreamers, Take Action.* Another trigger was hearing someone say that later in life, people usually don't regret what they did but what they didn't do. I do not want to have any regrets. Even if I had access to a crystal ball and it showed me that *The Apple and The Stone* would sell fewer than one copy, I would keep writing. I am determined to follow my dreams despite the many available excuses.

I simply do not want to have any regrets about not pursuing my dreams. Do you want to live with the regret of not at least trying? If your answer is *no*, I urge you to stop making excuses and start taking action. Do not let fear suffocate what you know you should do.

FIND YOUR OPPORTUNITIES IN YOUR OBSTACLES

Do some opposition and obstacle investigating today to locate evidence of opportunities in your personal or professional life. Remove trepidation and fear from your vision to better see where your opportunities are hidden. As Napoleon Hill said, "Your big opportunity may be right where you are now."[27]

There are opportunities hidden in our pain, failures, hardships, broken relationships, alcoholism, drug addiction, and whatever obstacles and Goliaths we encounter.

Merriam-Webster defines opportunity as *a favorable juncture of*

---

27. Napoleon Hill, *Your Big Opportunity May Be Right Where You Are Now*, BrainyQuote, accessed June 13, 2025, BrainyQuote.

circumstances—a good chance for advancement or progress.[28] The same dictionary defines obstacles as *something that makes movement or progress difficult.*[29] In other words, according to Merriam-Webster, obstacles and opportunities are complete opposites—one advances movement, and the other hinders movement. I disagree with their definition of obstacles somewhat. I view obstacles as *a seemingly unfavorable juncture of circumstances that, when viewed without fear, is an excellent chance for advancement or progress.*

Recall my ocean example: before boats, oceans seemed unfavorable for travel. It would seem outright suicidal to travel on water for significant distances (before boats). However, once fear was discarded, oceans became favorable for travel. Note that the oceans did not become less dangerous or even shallower. What changed? What was previously defined as an obstacle was now determined to be an opportunity, an excellent chance for advancement or progress. When you look at your obstacles with this understanding, your eyes will brighten with optimism, and your hopes will elevate with joy.

FIND AND EXECUTE OPPORTUNITIES EARLY IN THE OBSTACLE PROCESS

Risk increases when opportunities are not quickly found and quickly executed. In other words, the time it takes to recognize and seize opportunities in obstacles is directly proportional to the increase in risk. A small hole in a ship will eventually sink it if the shipwright fails to perform their duties correctly. It is also why a marriage can

---

28. Merriam-Webster, *Opportunity*, accessed June 26, 2025, https://www.merriam-webster.com/dictionary/opportunity.

29. Merriam-Webster, *Obstacle*, accessed June 26, 2025, https://www.merriam-webster.com/dictionary/obstacle.

fail after decades of minor issues not immediately seen and addressed. Time is of the essence when facing Goliath obstacles and opposition.

Apple might have been history if Steve Jobs had not seen and seized the opportunity to work with Microsoft when he did. Apple appeared to have been on a one-way collision course with disaster. It stands to reason that if another Apple executive had seen and executed this opportunity ten years earlier, when the obstacle was first encountered, Apple would likely have saved millions in legal fees and earned billions in revenue. Steve Jobs was not with Apple from 1985 to 1997; he had been fired.[30] Obstacles, opportunities, and the timing associated with each will determine the outcome.

Let's revisit the David and Goliath confrontation. When David first sees the giant and hears Goliath's thunderous voice echoing, Goliath is already an experienced warrior and army veteran with multiple campaigns in Gath and nearby areas.

Goliath wasn't born a giant; he was once a large embryo tucked inside his mother's womb. Still, he was a baby then. If Saul (or someone else) had defeated Goliath when he was a younger, fierce warrior, the giant wouldn't have seemed so unbeatable years later. It's best to face challenges early, while they are still small, so confront baby Goliaths before they grow out of control. Don't lose hope if your current challenges seem impossible.

David's victory over Goliath offers great hope for you and me. Whenever the odds seem heavily stacked against us, it's time to fight with confidence and faith.

Fight against discouragement, fight against depression, fight against giving up, fight against negative thoughts, and fight against doubt and

---

30. Isaacson, *Steve Jobs*, 307.

fear. Fight whatever obstacles and challenges you face. You have what it takes to be victorious. There is a David within you.

The moment David faced the giant, he was ready to fight.

He was prepared to fight because he had the necessary tools to battle the giant and faith in God. Steve Jobs was ready to fight after facing his Goliath firing because he saw opportunities to move forward using the stones of innovation. He also had funding, connections with friends, and knowledge of running a computer business. Importantly, he did not start a venture that was entirely foreign to him. He remained within the technological landscape. By doing so, he was able to draw on his personal experiences related to his expertise, and so did David, who used a stone. After all, our experiences should serve as the foundation upon which we build to reach new heights. *Never forget the lessons your pain, hardships, and obstacles have taught you.*

Assess your obstacles and recognize how they can propel you toward new opportunities. Challenges are not roadblocks—they are opportunity roadways. Do not panic, stress, or complain, because these negative emotions cloud your thinking and stall your progress.

Embracing challenges with confidence and a positive mindset can really push you closer to your dreams. Just start taking small steps today and stay focused on what you need to succeed. If you feel like you're missing some tools or knowledge, don't hesitate to reach out for help from educators, mentors, or friends. Remember, you've got the awareness of what's ahead and why quitting isn't an option. Be inspired by what David and Steve Jobs did: face the fight head-on with courage and determination!

STRATEGY 1 TAKEAWAYS

Saul and the Men in the Army	Steve Jobs and Teenager David
Saw an obstacle	Saw opportunity
Complained	Accepted the challenge
Reacted with stress	Responded with calm

YOUR TURN TO REFLECT AND ACT

1. What opportunities can you uncover within your challenges?

2. How will you move forward and make the best of them?

3. What practices will help you remain calm and centered under pressure?

Signature: _____ Today's date: _____

THE HEAD-ON FIGHT

Confront Your Issues and Fight for Resolution

He teacheth my hands to war, so that a bow
of steel is broken by mine arms.
DAVID

Apple became the world's most profitable company because Steve Jobs and another cofounder fought relentlessly for its survival and success. They believed deeply in their vision and refused to stop fighting for it.

Walter Isaacson writes that Steve Jobs and Steve Wozniak sold some of their belongings to raise funds to start Apple. Jobs sold his Volkswagen for $1,500, but two weeks later, the purchaser complained that the engine had a fault, so Jobs paid for half the repairs. Wozniak sold his HP calculator for $500, but then the purchaser scammed him out of $250. Then, to make matters worse, shortly after Apple was formed, the first partner, Ronald Wayne, got cold feet, withdrew his investment, and left. However, despite Apple's rough start, which was certainly filled with many obstacles and challenges, Steve Jobs and Steve Wozniak stayed committed to their dream. They prepared to fight. And they fought to keep the Apple dream alive.[31]

---

31. Isaacson, *Steve Jobs*, 60–64.

Wayne's 10% stake in Apple, which he sold for $800 in 1976, would be worth around $300 billion in 2025.[32] Concerns over financial risk drove his decision to leave, as he feared being personally liable for Apple's debts.[33] Despite Apple's staggering valuation—$3.172 trillion in 2025.[34] Wayne has stated that he does not regret his choice, believing the stress of staying with Apple would have been overwhelming.[35]

Steve Jobs's biographer Walter Isaacson noted that in 2013, Ronald Wayne was living alone in a small Nevada home. His income: social security and whatever he might have won from the penny slots in Nevada.[36] In a 2012 Facebook post, Ronald Wayne wrote that if he had known Apple would produce 300 millionaires within its first four years, he would not have left Apple when he did.[37]

One might argue had he known that supporting someone else's dream and helping them fight for it would have yielded such a great and quick reward, he would have kept fighting. For the record, I do not know Mr. Wayne, and I certainly do not want to sound like I am judging him because I am not. I am just stating the facts my research

---

32. Preston Fore, "Apple Cofounder Ronald Wayne Sold His 10% Stake for $800 in 1976—Today It'd Be Worth up to $300 Billion," *Fortune*, June 24, 2025, https://fortune.com/2025/06/24/apple-cofounder-ronald-wayne-sold-10-percent-stake-early-today-worth-300-billion-steve-jobs-steve-wozniak/.

33. Aasma Khan, "Ron Wayne: Apple's Forgotten Founder Who Walked Away," YourStory, April 10, 2025, https://yourstory.com/2025/04/ron-wayne-apple-founder-story.

34. "Top 10 Tech Companies by Market Cap 2025," *Financial Express*, May 3, 2025, https://www.financialexpress.com/trending/top-10-tech-companies-by-market-cap-2025-who-leads-globally-and-where-does-india-stand/3831051/.

35. Dave Manuel, "Why Did Ronald Wayne Sell His 10% Stake in Apple for Just $800?" *DaveManuel.com*, January 23, 2024, https://www.davemanuel.com/2024/01/23/ronald-wayne-shares-sold-apple/.

36. Isaacson, Steve Jobs, 65-66.

37. Ronald G. Wayne, "Why I Left Apple Computer After Only 12 Days," Facebook post, February 22, 2012, quoted in *Mac History*, February 23, 2012, https://www.mac-history.net/2012/02/23/ron-wayne-why-i-left-apple-computer-after-only-12-days/.

uncovered. I have also learned that assisting others without the promise of personal rewards results in a tremendous feeling of gratification.

HELP OTHERS WIN THEIR FIGHT

Helping someone with their struggles or fights is generally a good idea. Life is such that everyone, at some point, needs assistance. Help isn't always monetary; we each can help in various ways. It may come as an encouraging word or a smile. It could involve standing up to a bully at school, online, in the workplace, or by reporting the situation to a trusted authority. You might need to actively participate in the fight against injustice and discrimination toward those who don't look like you or share your beliefs. Assisting in rectifying any wrongs is valuable help.

You may need to fight using the fists of forgiveness, love, and patience to save a drug-addicted teenager. You may need to fight by not giving up on your child or someone else's child. You may need to help fight for someone else's dream by paying for their education or schoolbooks. You will feel great knowing you made or tried to make a positive difference in someone's life. Furthermore, helping someone advance their dream might advance your dream as well.

YOU NEED TO FIGHT FOR YOURSELF
BEFORE YOU CAN FIGHT FOR OTHERS

A long time ago, I recall being asked: "*If there was a loss of pressure in the airplane, would you put on your oxygen mask first or your baby's mask?*" This was such an easy question with such an obvious answer that I must have chuckled. "*Of course, I would put the baby's mask on first,*" was my pompous reply.

My thought was that the baby's lungs were not as strong as mine, so I needed to put on the baby's oxygen mask first. To my embarrassment and dismay, I was told my answer was incorrect. I should have put on my mask first, and then the baby's mask. From this, I concluded that you must fight for yourself before you can effectively fight for others.

FIGHT FOR YOURSELF

Fighting for your dreams is not anyone else's battle but yours. Do not wait for permission, validation, or another champion to clear the path—step forward and fight. You alone hold the power to chase your vision, shape your destiny, and forge the way ahead. No one else can take the fighter's seat in your journey.

> Fighting for your dreams is not anyone else's battle but yours. Do not wait for permission, validation, or another champion to clear the path, step forward and fight.

Grip the wheel. Set the course. Move forward with relentless determination.

Fight in the rain, fight in the cold, and fight through bruises and setbacks. Confront disappointments, pain, regret, and unforgiveness, not as barriers, but as battles worth overcoming.

Fight for a future greater than today. Fight for yourself, your children, and your family. You owe it to them. You owe it to yourself. And when doubt creeps in, fight anyway.

You were born and are still alive because the globe awaits you to add your mark. You have a purpose. None of us knows whether our efforts (our fights) will result in more wins than losses or draws.

Regardless, you must fight. Win, lose, or draw, fight. When life knocks you down, get up and fight. If you are too tired to stand and fight, crawl and fight.

You can never overcome life's challenges if you do not fight. One of my favorite quotes is from famed hockey player Wayne Gretzky: *"You will miss 100 percent of the shots you don't take."*[38] Wouldn't it be better to have taken the shot and missed rather than wondering years later, what if I had taken it? What if I had given more effort? What might I have accomplished had I just done XYZ or PQR? What if I had not given up at all?

Basketball icon Michael Jordan won six NBA championships with the Chicago Bulls. He also won several MVP awards. Undoubtedly, his skills played a significant role in his and his team's numerous accomplishments. However, none of his basketball achievements would have been possible if he had not shot the ball when he had opportunities. And guess what? You might find it difficult to believe that Michael Jordan missed many shots.

Yes, the same Michael Jordan who is often called the greatest basketball player of all time. In words attributed to him: *I've missed over 9,000 shots in my career. I've lost nearly 300 games. Twenty-six times, I've been trusted to take the winning shot and missed. I've failed time and again throughout my life. And this is why I succeed.*[39]

Michael Jordan showcased incredible basketball talent, but it's important to remember that his legendary status also came from his willingness to take the tough shots. Similarly, someone might have

---

38. Wayne Gretzky, *99: My Life in Pictures* (Toronto: Mint Publishers, 2000), quoted in "TOP 25 Quotes by Wayne Gretzky," *A-Z Quotes,* accessed June 30, 2025, https://www.azquotes.com/author/5901-Wayne_Gretzky.

39. Michael Jordan, quoted in Robert Goldman and Stephen Papson, *Nike Culture: The Sign of the Swoosh* (Thousand Oaks, CA: SAGE Publications, 1998), 49.

the most beautiful soprano voice, but if they're too afraid to sing, they're on par with someone like me who can't sing at all.

Does having a great voice matter if you don't use it? Plant the seeds of your dreams and plant them well. Water them with hard work, fertilize them with resilience, care for them daily with encouragement, and you will watch them flourish. If the prize is worth it to you and your future, you must fight to earn it. Please do not stop fighting. Many have lost out on great rewards because they gave up. Some fights may go unnecessarily longer than expected, but you owe it to yourself to keep on fighting if you want to win at life and achieve your dreams.

COMPLETING THE REQUIREMENT
OF A FOUR-YEAR DEGREE

It took me 21 years to complete my bachelor's degree. Imagine that. I was 42 when I attained a bachelor's degree. A degree that should have taken me four years or less took me over two decades to finish. Making foolish decisions such as switching schools three times, switching majors, and losing credits were contributing factors. In addition, I took out more student loans than I needed. This hurt when a portion of my then $276/week paycheck was garnished because I could not make the minimum monthly student loan payments.

My excuses for not being able to make these payments had ruptured the forbearance patience limit of the Federal Student Loan authority. They were on to me. I refused to answer their calls or respond to their letters for months, which exacerbated the issue. But I was resolute in attaining a college degree to position myself better to attain my dreams. As such, I kept fighting to earn that bachelor's degree.

As a result of continuously fighting for my future, I completed not only a bachelor's degree but also a master's degree and a PhD, and I am still learning today. Indeed, a person does not need a college degree to write a book. However, I doubt I would have had the discipline, skill, and willpower to pen this book without the extremely mentally challenging PhD experience.

WILL YOURSELF TO FIGHT FOR YOUR DREAMS UNTIL YOU ACHIEVE THEM

This is my first book. I will write it to the best of my ability and plan to finish it within six months. No matter what life throws at me, and regardless of how I may feel at times, I vow to continue writing until I place the last period.

I'll write when I am happy, I'll write when I'm sad, through moments of joy and the trials I've had. I'll write through the storms and when life becomes still, with pen in my grip and a fire in my will. I'll tap on the keys till my burdens are gone and pour out purpose from midnight till dawn. I'll write through the silence, I'll write through the strain. I'll write until no words in me remain.

Please forgive me, a sudden rush of poetic inspiration overwhelmed my mind. If I can write a book, I know beyond a shadow of a doubt that your wildest dreams are within your grasp.

Maybe you have not completely followed the paths to some of your dreams. Life may have gotten in the way. But no worries, the fact that you are reading this book means you are still alive. And since you are still alive, your dreams are still attainable. I believe in you and your dreams. Do you believe in yourself and your dreams? If so, now is the best time to restart walking to your dreams. Now is the best time to begin taking shots at your dreams. Now is the best time to reignite passion and fight for your dreams.

DAVID ASKS THE COMPELLING QUESTION

When David arrives at the war zone, Goliath has been challenging Saul and his army for forty days, yet no one dares to fight him. Goliath's thundering voice threatens to register on the Richter scale as he bellows for a man from the Israelite army to fight him. Goliath states that if he wins, the Israelites will become slaves to the Philistines. Conversely, if the Israelite fighters win, the Philistines will be enslaved by the Israelites.[40] A lot is at stake.

David hears Goliath's threats and asks soldiers standing close by what the prize is for killing Goliath. The soldiers say that Saul would enrich the man with great riches, give him his daughter as wife, and make his family live tax-free forever.[41]

His oldest brother Eliab overhears him and becomes furious. He scolds David angrily, questioning what he is doing on the battlefield and who is caring for the sheep he was told to watch. Before David can respond, Eliab says he knows David is a troublemaker, just there to check out the fight.[42] At that moment, Eliab has no idea he will soon witness his brother in action in the main event.

Without arguing with his oldest brother, David, asks him two questions: *What have I done now? Is there not a cause?*[43] He then turns away from Eliab and calmly asks the other soldiers about the prize again, as if seeking confirmation.[44] David's determination propels the soldiers to tell Saul about him, and the army chief summons him.[45]

---

40. *KJV*, 1 Samuel 17:9.
41. *KJV*, 1 Samuel 17:25-27.
42. *KJV*, 1 Samuel 17:28.
43. *KJV*, 1 Samuel 17:29.
44. *KJV*, 1 Samuel 17:30.
45. *KJV*, 1 Samuel 17:31.

Recall, this was Saul and the army's fight. It was a professional fight between grown military men. Saul and his men were trained to fight. It was their job to fight. It was their responsibility to fight. It was their duty to fight. They needed to fight.

However, when qualified fighters fail to fight, non-traditional fighters become a threat to their jobs. When business leaders and team leaders fail to lead, less qualified candidates become a threat to their positions. It is interesting to note that Saul would lose his position as king and commander-in-chief to David several years later. This is mainly because Saul refused to fight when he should have fought.

Is there not a cause to fight for your dreams? Isn't your life worth fighting for? Isn't your health worth fighting for? Isn't your job worth fighting for? Aren't your goals worth fighting for? Isn't your family worth fighting for? Isn't your happiness worth fighting for? Isn't living a stress-free life worth fighting for?

Whatever you consider valuable is worth your fight. Fight for it with every fiber of your being. Fight. Fight. Fight. Again, expect obstacles, opposition, and challenges. Learn to identify them, look for opportunities, and then get your mental gloves and fight. Since no one can effectively fight against what he or she does not see, one must be able to identify the correct enemy. Some enemies are obvious. But some are hard to see, especially when their current form is a baby Goliath.

IDENTIFY THE ENEMIES OF YOUR DREAMS AND FIGHT THEM

I dislike being the bearer of not-so-good news, but you have enemies everywhere. Enemies surround us. Now, before you start looking out your windows, locking your doors, and rushing to call 911, 119, 191,

999, or whichever applicable emergency country code is needed for your geographic location, let's identify some of our enemies.

You must be your own police and military, but don't worry; you've got this. Please realize your enemies are not all the same. However, they all have the same intent.

Remember, your enemies aim to harm your dreams, often starting by planting negative thoughts in your mind. The real battle to protect your dreams begins within your own thoughts. If you don't win this mental fight, these negative influences can spread throughout your whole being, affecting your future in ways you don't want. Stay strong and positive and keep your dreams safe!

Let's look at some of these enemies and see how we can effectively eliminate them before they ruin our dreams. You will notice that some of them are self-created, self-fed, or self-embraced. Nevertheless, it's important to expose and defeat them. To achieve this, you need to know their whereabouts. Often, our most formidable enemy resides in our minds. Many of life's battles are fought and decided in the mind. To succeed in life, you must first prevail in your mind.

NEGATIVE THOUGHTS

Negative thoughts are the number one universal dream killer. You could be the most beautiful woman on the planet, but if you constantly open the door of your mind to negative thoughts that you are not beautiful, you will likely never enter a beauty pageant. And if you entered, could you (really) win? If you won, you might question why you won, thinking you didn't deserve to win.

You might even convince yourself the pageant was rigged. People may try to convince you of your beauty, but you will never see yourself as beautiful until you discipline your thoughts to believe it. Let me add that beauty is more internal than external. The most beautiful person might not win a beauty pageant. Please forgive me for digressing here. The richest people are not usually those with the largest bank accounts.

Anyway, if you possess the most physically intimidating strength available yet are convinced in your mind you are weak, you will never experience your true strength. If you do not fight the negative thoughts that whisper you are not strong and that everyone else is stronger than you, you will never reach your full potential and fulfill your dreams. In his best-selling book *The Power of Positive Thinking*, Norman Vincent Peale writes that people who constantly think they are not good enough will have difficulty realizing their dreams.[46]

Are you battling negative thoughts? Did a parent, spouse, family member, or coworker ever make you feel you were not good enough? Do you think you are not smart because you did not finish high school? Do you think you are not smart because of difficulty getting a job or promotion?

Your thoughts determine your perspective and result in your actions. Saul thought he was no match for Goliath; therefore, he lived in fear and uncertainty. He never allowed his mind to connect with courage and deliver a solution. As a result, he lost the battle without physical fighting. Don't give up before you enter the ring.

Maybe you are divorced and feel your self-worth has bottomed out. Alternatively, maybe you are not yet married and are convinced that something is wrong with you and that you do not deserve to be happily married. Could the issue be the negative thoughts affecting

---

46. Norman Vincent Peale, *The Power of Positive Thinking* (Englewood Cliffs, NJ: Prentice Hall, 1952), see especially chapters 1–3.

how you truly see yourself? Negative thoughts often abound regardless of the nature of your dreams and hopes.

Have negative thoughts captured and imprisoned your dreams?

If yes, do not let this be a life sentence. Your dreams are begging you to free them. Free them of the negative thoughts that bind them.

FIGHT AND DESTROY NEGATIVE THOUGHTS

Now that you are fully aware that negative thoughts kill dreams, what will you do about them? Did you say, "Kill them?" If so, you are correct. Yes, kill them, destroy them, annihilate them. Believe it or not, fighting and eliminating negative thoughts is possible. You can do it. However, you must be committed, disciplined, and persevere in combating your negative thoughts and beliefs about yourself and your abilities.

To achieve this, Norman Vincent Peale suggests you can overcome negative thought patterns by replacing them with positive and uplifting thoughts. He encourages you to affirm yourself through writing and speaking positive affirmations regularly. With consistent effort and determination, he believes your thoughts will shift to a positive outlook, helping you reach the goals of your dreams.

Author and transformational coach Lisa Nichols added that we must begin transforming by exposing our lies. She states that the lies we tell ourselves keep us down and limit our movement to significant accomplishments. In her sessions with clients, she asks them to list, in pencil, all the lies they believe or tell themselves about money, relationships, abilities, and more. Then, they write the corresponding truth beneath each lie using a red pen. They read each lie and truth aloud four times daily for the next two days. According to Nichols, this exercise empowers people to train their brains using neuro-linguistic programming. Her clients are then instructed to erase the lies.

If this exercise is done correctly, Nichols states our brain will default to the truth when faced with the lies we used to tell ourselves. She also underscores the importance of affirming yourself daily.[47]

I agree 100 percent. You need to reaffirm yourself every day, every morning, every night before going to bed, and even when you get up at night to use the bathroom. Remind yourself that you are beautiful, worthy of love, and a winner. You will achieve your dreams if you work hard to achieve them. Leave little notes of these affirmations in your pocketbooks, wallet, car, bed, bathroom mirror, and workstation or cubicle if needed.

If you are struggling with thoughts of low self-esteem, go a step further and place your affirmation notes in your underwear drawer. This way, you can see and read them when the negative thoughts are likely most active.

If negative thoughts are not a significant issue for you or are not the main issue seeking to kill your dreams, your enemy might be procrastination. Yes, negative thoughts have a distant cousin named procrastination. It does not visit as often as negative thoughts but always seems to show up when there is a task you need to accomplish.

PROCRASTINATION

Procrastination is not just a delay; it is a silent thief, stealing moments of progress before you notice. It lurks in hesitation, disguising itself as caution, convincing you that there will always be more time, a better moment, another opportunity down the road. But time waits for no one, and every postponed step adds to a mountain of missed chances.

---

47. Lisa Nichols, "The Secret to More Happiness, Success, & Wellness," *The Model Health Show*, hosted by Shawn Stevenson, episode 773, accessed June 15, 2025, https://themodelhealthshow. com/happiness-success-wellness/.

Procrastination immobilizes you and keeps dreams locked in thought rather than action. It injects fear and doubt to seep into spaces meant for movement. It does not strike in obvious ways; it works subtly, chips away at confidence, and whispers excuses that sound reasonable but lead to stagnation. If left unchecked, it kills momentum, shatters consistency, slowly dismantles progress, and leaves you with regrets.

Procrastination is a quiet and clever enemy disguised as hesitation, fueled by excuses, and determined to steal your progress. Stop waiting. Start moving.

Procrastination is a quiet and clever enemy disguised as hesitation, fueled by excuses, and determined to steal your progress. Stop waiting. Start moving. It often acts like it really cares about your well-being. For instance, it frequently whispers gently in your ears, transmitting seemingly sweet words and likable statements such as "*You can do that tomorrow*" or "*You know you need more sleep.*" Interestingly, for some reason, it always seems to know when there is something important you need to accomplish. Yet it will justify you needing to put off that task, whispering you can't afford to miss watching the latest episode of your favorite show. Of course, you do not want to be left out of the conversation at school or work the following day.

Procrastination often tells high school and college students, "*You can do your homework later,*" or "*You can study later after you play your favorite video game,*" or "*Check out what's happening on Facebook, Tik-Tok, Snap, or IG.*" It knows very well you'll be tired after a social media rendezvous. Procrastination will assert, "*You got this; you have enough time to work on your presentation,*" even though you know you really don't. You realize "Procs" (as it loves to be called) is no good for you, but you keep seeing and spending valuable time with it because it makes you feel so good. Hmm, well, if you don't mind me stating the obvious, then please listen to me.

Procrastination (or Procs) is your enemy. Its sole purpose is to waste your time, delay your actions, and cause you to miss the flight to your dreams. Procrastination is a cunningly sweet talker. How do you deal with it best? How do you prevent it from stagnating your progress and killing your dreams?

DEFEAT PROCRASTINATION

You must sever your relationship with procrastination before it severs the connection to your dream. This is easier said than done because of the underlying psychological attachments causing people to procrastinate. In other words, you might know you need to stop procrastinating but find it extremely difficult. Dr. Neil A. Fiore, who wrote *The Now Habit: A Strategic Program for Overcoming Procrastination and Enjoying Guilt-Free Play*, noted that procrastination imprisons people in a harsh cycle. He disagrees with the notion that people procrastinate because they are lazy.[48]

Dr. Fiore explained that people procrastinate because of underlying issues such as low self-esteem, fear of failure, indecisiveness, and negative self-thoughts. He notes that people must fight the underlying mental problems to remedy this and defeat procrastination. He asserts that when procrastinators think positively, they feel confident and act decisively.

48. Neil A. Fiore, *The Now Habit: A Strategic Program for Overcoming Procrastination and Enjoying Guilt-Free Play* (New York: Penguin Group, 2007), 5–6.

As with fighting and killing negative thoughts, the battle with procrastination must begin in your mind; change your thoughts and attitude. Your actions will follow suit once your thoughts and attitudes are positively changed. Your thoughts will drive your actions. If you believe a task is too difficult, you might delay doing it. However, if you think you can accomplish the task and will feel great about the accomplishment, you are unlikely to procrastinate.

Basketball players who believe they are talented and can make a game-winning shot will confidently shoot the ball. These players will seek the opportunity to win the game. If the player misses, they will practice even harder and look forward to the next chance to hit a game-winning shot.

On the other hand, a player lacking confidence will not want the ball when the game is on the line. Giving such a player the ball when the game is on the line is not usually a good idea. If the player does not make the shot, his or her lack of confidence will sink even lower. And because the person does not positively think about himself or herself, then self-doubt, low self-esteem, feelings of unworthiness, and incompetence will take root, grow, and strangle his or her basketball dreams.

Keep shooting the ball of life. Stop letting procrastination weigh you down and slow your journey to accomplishing your goals. Stay consistent and move forward with urgency; there are obstacles to overcome before you can fully achieve your dreams.

CREDIT CARD DEBT

Bad credit card debt is a dream killer. It aims to shackle and restrict your journey to your dreams financially. Bad credit card debt may be defined as unnecessary spending or buying things you do not need.

This results in people working extra jobs, being stressed out, and not having quality time to live a rewarding and fulfilling life.

Don't get me wrong, credit cards are okay if used responsibly. However, many Americans struggle with credit card debt, which has trapped them. According to the Federal Reserve Bank, credit card debt reached $1.17 trillion in the fourth quarter of 2024.[49]

If high credit card balances are your Goliath, the consensus is to strike smart: aim your stone at the highest-interest debts first, then shift remaining balances to a lower-rate card, slashing interest and fees.[50]

It will be beneficial to use credit cards responsibly. Taking these actions will free you of stress and free up money to fund your dreams. Avoid hindrances by taking the steps necessary to ride the road to your goals. Also, rid yourself of the doubts from others that sap and weaken the energy of your dreams.

Stop procrastinating and fight against the Goliaths that challenge you and whose aim is to destroy you. It does not matter whether they are small or large; fight until you succeed.

49. Federal Reserve Bank of New York, *Quarterly Report on Household Debt and Credit*, Center for Microeconomic Data, Q4 2024, accessed June 15, 2025, https://www.newyorkfed.org/microeconomics/hhdc.html

50. Marianne Hayes, "Paying Off Debt With the Highest APR vs. Highest Balance," *Experian*, April 19, 2024, https://www.experian.com/blogs/ask-experian/should-i-pay-off-highest-balance-or-highest-interest-first/.

STRATEGY 2 TAKEAWAYS

Saul and the Men in the Army	Steve Jobs and Teenager David
Refused to fight	Chose to fight
Lacked commitment to success	Committed fully to succeeding
Procrastinated	Acted with urgency and focus

YOUR TURN TO REFLECT AND ACT

1. How will you stand up and fight the Goliaths in your life?

2. What daily habits show your true commitment to success?

3. What steps will you take to eliminate procrastination and take decisive action?

Signature: _____ Today's date: _____

THE CLOSED EAR

Don't Let Doubt and Doubters Derail Your Dreams

> *Your time is limited, so don't waste it living someone else's*
> *life. Don't be trapped by dogma—which is living with the*
> *result of other people's thinking. Don't let the noise of other's*
> *opinions drown out your inner voice. And most important,*
> *have the courage to follow your heart and intuition.*
>
> **STEVE JOBS**

avid suddenly finds himself face to face with Saul, the king and army chief, the seasoned warrior. His words fluctuate Saul's blood pressure. David tells Saul not to suffer heart failure because he has accepted the challenge and will fight the giant.[51]

Saul tells David he is out-of-his-mind-crazy for even thinking he can fight Goliath, much less win. What did David think, Saul wondered? Did the boy think he and the soldiers feared Goliath for no plausible reason? Saul wondered if David had trouble with his eyes. He heard that when people get older, they usually need glasses, but the youngster certainly appeared to need magnifying glasses. Saul, the father figure and army commander, authoritatively counsels the

---

51. *KJV*, 1 Samuel 17:32

youngster to be rational. The reasons Saul gives are on point, they are true.

Saul cautions David that he is an inexperienced young man without any military training or combat experience, noting that Goliath had fought in battles at David's age. Goliath had been a successful fighter long before David's parents began dating. Saul even feared telling David what he had seen Goliath do to his enemies; he utterly destroys them.

Saul, the army leader, tells David, the young man, that his lack of fighting experience makes him unable to defeat Goliath. The giant's record vividly fills Saul's mind, terrifyingly confirming his deadly accomplishments. This evidence leaves the army leader with no doubt that David cannot beat the giant.

Saul concludes that David was neither skilled nor experienced enough to fight and slay the monstrous giant. This pattern continues today. Even now, many in leadership roles still doubt others' abilities. They sometimes underestimate those who could help lead them to victory.

When my son Aaron played high school football, he was a standout player, breaking and setting numerous records. He was tagged as one of the 100 best football players in the region and diligently worked hard to attain a scholarship to play football at the Division I (DI) level. This is the highest level in American collegiate sports. The next two lower levels are DII and DIII.

During his junior and high school senior years, he and I sent his highlight film to over 125 coaches. However, no DI scholarship offers came. The closest we got during these years was one offer to be a preferred walk-on. This meant he would be on the team but not initially on a scholarship. He declined. He felt he worked exceptionally hard and was good enough to play collegiate football at the highest level, the DI level.

During his senior year in high school, we met with his head coach to create a plan. During the meeting, the coach asked him why he wanted to play Division I football. My son explained that he worked hard and believed he could compete at the Division I level. The coach asked, "*Why do you think you haven't received any Division I scholarship offers?*" My son shrugged. His coach replied, "*Maybe you aren't as good as you think.*" The coach suggested a few Division III schools where he felt my son would be a better fit. As we left the meeting, Aaron declared that he would give up the game if he didn't receive a Division I scholarship offer to play football. I cautioned him against such a firm stance because I knew how much he loved football.

After playing his final season, he still did not receive any DI scholarship offers. After much research, my wife and I decided to have him apply to a prep school for a four-month football program where he would undoubtedly get more exposure than he received in our small town in New York. Despite a less than 9 percent acceptance rate, Aaron was accepted to Milford Academy, one of the top prep schools in the Northeast, solely based on his high school football film and passing an interview.

Milford Academy won all 11 games in the 2016 season when Aaron played there.[52] I was told this was only the second unbeaten season in their 100-year existence. Within one week of the season finishing, Aaron received a full scholarship to play at the DII level. My wife and I were elated. Gratitude and excitement suddenly took up residence in our home.

---

52. Milford Academy, *2016 Football Schedule*, accessed June 16, 2025, https://www.milfordacademy. org/athletics-schedule-2016.html.

This school was a six-and-a-half-hour drive from our home, so we would be able to drive to the games. More importantly, he would get a fully paid education. However, the plan was for my son to delay signing with the school in case he received a DI scholarship. He continued to dream about getting what he wanted, a DI scholarship. This was in December 2016, so we knew we had some time before signing day.

College football signing day in the US is the first Wednesday in February. We had time before committing to the DII School. Oh boy, were we wrong.

In January 2017, I contacted one of Milford's coaches. I asked if my son should go ahead and sign at the DII School or if there was a possibility he would get a DI offer. The coach asked one question, and his question caught me off guard. "*How did the visit go?*"

"*What visit?*" I asked.

His slow and measured response gave me pause and sent chills up my spine: "*Maybe you need to talk to your son.*" I immediately asked Aaron about this visit. He nonchalantly responded that the recruiting coach from the DII School had offered him an official visit. An official visit is where the school pays for the athlete and parents to visit and tour the school. Unbelievably, he never mentioned the official visit to my wife and me.

Without requesting his explanation, I immediately had my son call the DII coach to apologize and to see if the scholarship was still on the table. It wasn't. The coach responded that he could apply in the fall (August). They had offered him the scholarship to begin in Spring 2017.

At this point, it was clear that he had lost the only scholarship he had been offered (valued at approximately $140,000). The original excitement and gratitude balloons that so beautifully danced in our home suddenly popped with a deafening sound of disappointment and anger. I felt my heart drop. Disbelief, disappointment, and outrage followed.

I was livid. I explained to him in no uncertain terms that he was wrong and unfair to both his mom and me when he decided on his own to lose his only football scholarship offer. He apologized, then calmly said, "*Don't worry, Dad, God will give me a DI offer.*"

Something about the calmness and confidence with which he made the statement gave me pause. I timidly replied, "*Okay, if you believe God will grant you a DI scholarship, I will believe with you.*" Four weeks later, he received a full DI scholarship to Central Connecticut State University, two hours from our home.

His high school coach implied he was not good enough to play at the DI level. The coach doubted his ability and suggested he settle for less than his dream. Aaron's faith in God and his dream were the differences in his playing DI football.

I should also note he didn't just make the football team in 2017; he started some games in his first year. Months later, the team won its first Northeast Conference (NEC) championship in seven years and set a school record by winning eight straight games in a single season in 2017. Additionally, they earned their first-ever FCS playoff spot in school history after finishing last place in 2016, when they only won two games. In October 2018, Aaron broke four DI football records and was featured on ESPN's Sports Center and another program.[53]

---

53. ESPN News Services, "CCSU's Aaron Dawson Sets Record with 308 Rushing Yards in a Half," *ESPN*, October 28, 2018, https://www.espn.com/college-football/story/_/id/25101020/ccsu-aaron-dawson-sets-record-308-rushing-yards-half.

Never doubt yourself and your abilities,
no matter who doubts you.

Aaron wouldn't have won a DI championship in his freshman year or broken DI records if he had doubted himself as his high school coach did. Never doubt yourself and your abilities, no matter who doubts you.

Like Saul, Goliath also believes David isn't strong enough to defeat him. In fact, Goliath is stunned when he sees his challenger. The giant's massive frame shakes with bewilderment and rage. He feels disrespected. His boisterous grunt frightens and disrupts nearby birds in their V formation, causing them to change into a Z formation. Goliath looks on in disbelief when he sees his young and much smaller opponent. He is sure King Saul had lost his mind. The giant loudly mutters, "*What the hell is going on?*" Big, strong men were terrified of him. He bullied and bulldozed anyone who crossed his path. *Who the heck is this little punk?*

At the same time, David's brothers are consumed with shock. Dismay pressed their heads low and hollowed their hearts. Eliab, Abinadab, and Shammah, begin wondering how they would manage to scoop up his body parts after Goliath shredded their little brother to bits. They scream in their brother's ears, "*Are you crazy? What are you doing?*" They wonder what they will tell their father about what happened to his youngest son after Goliath shreds him to pieces.

They have no confidence whatsoever in David's chances of killing Goliath. They think he is crazy to even think about fighting the giant. What was David thinking if they, being his older brothers, thought they could not fight Goliath and win? Maybe he was becoming like the sheep for which he often cared—dumb.

It is always unfortunate and disheartening when those who are closest to you are often the ones who doubt you the most. It is even more painful when it comes from those who share your DNA. The ones who should believe, support, and encourage you are often your most prominent critics.

The obvious lesson here is you must continue to believe in yourself and in achieving your goals even when family members and close friends think your dreams are crazy and unattainable. Refuse to abandon your dreams because of others' short-sighted views of you.

If anyone should have volunteered and accepted Goliath's challenge, it should have been Saul, the king and CEO of the Israelite army. He was likely a giant, described as the tallest person in Israel years earlier.[54] Additionally, Saul had war experience and was very familiar with Goliath, so why didn't he think he could have fought and killed Goliath? If lack of experience was David's disqualification, what was Saul's continued excuse for not attempting to fight Goliath?

Could Saul have felt threatened by David's confidence? Could Saul have been scared that David might succeed in killing Goliath? Obviously, this would be embarrassing. Saul, the head of the army, and all his soldiers were terrified of the enemy Goliath, yet the boy was not afraid. Saul might have even wondered why David's three older brothers feared Goliath, but their youngest brother did not. Likely, Saul thought there was too much risk in sending the inexperienced boy against the experienced Goliath.

There was a lot at stake because Goliath had set the prize. If he won, the Israelites would be enslaved to the Philistines. Conversely, if for some inexplicable and implausible reason, the Israelites won,

---

54. *KJV*, 1 Samuel 9:2

the Philistines would become the Israelites' slaves. The stakes were enormous. Not to mention, the fighter who lost the fight would also lose his life.

Saul weighs the risks and concludes that no one, not him, nor any of his soldiers, and certainly not David, could fight and defeat the champion Philistine. Nonetheless, David saw it differently and liked the prizes Saul offered to the one who slew the giant.

Saul's prizes for the man who killed Goliath included his daughter in marriage and great riches. In addition, the victor's family would be exempt from paying taxes forever.[55] You can imagine that Saul's daughter had to be beautiful to be the main prize. She must have been finer than sugar and sweeter than honey.

There is no way Saul would (or could) have offered his daughter to persuade a man to seriously risk his life, unless the daughter could have won the Miss World pageant. She had to be gorgeous. No doubt, Saul's soldiers fantasized about what it would be like to enjoy the company of the young damsel. Nevertheless, the thought of fighting Goliath froze those thoughts in fear.

The rewards for killing Goliath were huge—but the risks were too great. Despite Saul's generous offers, none of his soldiers dared to risk their lives. They knew Goliath was the real threat. Others had tried and failed to bring down this beast of a man, this freak of nature.

For David, the fight was well worth the prizes. Perhaps he wasn't even fighting for the prizes listed. According to the Biblical account, David believed Goliath was dishonoring the Israelites, their God, and he needed to put a stop to it.[56] Since no one else took up the challenge, he was left to silence the Giant. It did not matter to David that

---

55. *KJV*, 1 Samuel 17:25
56. *KJV*, 1 Samuel 17:26

Saul felt he could not fight and kill Goliath. It also did not matter to David that his brothers did not believe in his abilities.

No one in the war zone believed David could defeat Goliath except David himself. Yet he stood firm, grounded in faith: faith in his God and in the gifts he carried. He refused to accept the limits others placed on him. Like David, Steve Jobs also faced fierce skeptics, but he too pressed forward with belief, in his vision, and in his ability to bring it to life.

STEVE JOBS'S DOUBTERS

In 1997, ten years after being fired from Apple, he made his return. The company was losing vast amounts of money, and its future appeared bleak. There were industry heavyweights who doubted Steve Jobs's ability and his dream of turning Apple into a successful, competitive company. Yet, Jobs had faith in his ability to make Apple profitable. He remained optimistic about turning the company's fortunes around. But his detractors publicly expressed their own professional opinions. In late 1997, Michael Dell, CEO of Dell Computers, was asked at a trade show what he would do if he were in Jobs's position. According to biographer Walter Isaacson, Dell said he would dissolve Apple and return the money to its shareholders. [57]

In Mr. Dell's opinion, Steve Jobs was incapable of achieving his goal of turning Apple into a profitable company. Mr. Dell was undoubtedly wrong. Decades later, we can see that Michael Dell is still wrong. I noted earlier that Forbes listed Apple as the world's top tech company in market capitalization, while Dell was outside the top ten companies.

---

57. Isaacson, *Steve Jobs*, 334.

Microsoft founder Bill Gates also had doubts about Steve Jobs's ability to turn Apple into a worthwhile Microsoft competitor. The *Huffington Post* reported that in 1998, Bill Gates expressed his bewilderment about why Steve Jobs wanted his CEO job back at Apple (after being fired). According to the report, Gates stated Jobs should be aware that he could not win with Apple.[58] Almost 30 years later, Apple is still ahead and winning against Microsoft in the race for the world's most profitable tech company.

Did Michael Dell and Bill Gates purposely err in their statements, doubting Steve Jobs's ability to turn around Apple? No. In fact, it made sense to them and others as well. These two men would not have gone on public record to make such extremely bold statements if they did not believe them to be true. They were certain Steve Jobs was making a huge mistake by thinking he could save Apple. Dell and Gates felt strongly that Steve Jobs would fail; both were embarrassingly wrong.

Michael Dell is obviously a very smart and competent leader. His founding and tremendous growth of Dell Computers from his college dorm speak volumes.[59] The troubling financial report he read and heard about Apple, showing the company in deep financial trouble, propelled him to state that he would have dissolved Apple if he had been the CEO.

Now, let's delve a little deeper into this scenario. Michael Dell would have had a lot of financial information about Apple. Apple was a public company then, meaning its extreme financial woes were

58. Bianca Bosker, "Bill Gates On Steve Jobs In 1998: 'He Knows He Can't Win' (AUDIO)," *HuffPost*, June 12, 2010, https://www.huffpost.com/entry/bill-gates-on-steve-jobs_n_533817.

59. Aparna Sahu, "Michael Dell's Journey: From Dorm Room to Tech Titan," *The Entrepreneur Story*, June 25, 2024, https://theentrepreneurstory.com/business/michael-dells-journey-from-dorm-room-to-tech-titan/.

public knowledge. This is likely the foundation on which Mr. Dell built his bold statement. No doubt, others shared the same sentiment that Apple was unlikely to rise from its bed of financial affliction.

Steve Jobs was knowledgeable about Apple's financial condition. In fact, he would have been privy to more intimate details about Apple's dark forecast. Nevertheless, he did not see Apple through the eyes of Michael Dell or accept his outlook. Michael Dell saw a rotting Apple that needed to be discarded. Steve Jobs saw an Apple needing preservatives; *The Jobs's Preservative*. And the Apple cofounder was 100 percent right.

How about you? Have others seen and declared your future to be bleak or dead? Have folks told you they would quit and give up if they were you? Has anyone mentioned that having a General Educational Development (GED) indicates you cannot successfully run a company? A GED is equivalent to a high school diploma in the USA.[60]

I am a college professor and a huge proponent of education; however, a lack of education should not stop you from graduating with your dreams. It is okay to hear others' opinions. But their opinions should be questioned if they are misaligned with your dreams, passion, and what you know about your capabilities. Their opinions may just be noise to quiet your dreams.

Like Michael Dell, Bill Gates is a brilliant and competent man. His founding, leadership, and the tremendous growth of Microsoft are proof. His proclamation that Steve Jobs and Apple would not win against him and Microsoft was not a skillful statement. Obviously, Gates did not have the vision Jobs had. Bill Gates saw the "now," while Steve Jobs saw the "then;" his bright future.

---

60. GED Testing Service, *Home – GED*, accessed June 23, 2025, https://www.ged.com

Do not let today's struggles define tomorrow's success. Where you stand now is not your final destination, keep believing forward.

Your present circumstances do not define your destiny. Struggles are temporary, setbacks are lessons, and obstacles are stepping stones—not roadblocks. Do not let today's struggles define tomorrow's success. Where you stand now is not your final destination, keep believing forward. The most significant transformations emerge from the toughest seasons. Your future is shaped not by where you are today, but by how boldly you step into tomorrow. Rise above doubt. Defy discouragement and unlock the greatness waiting within you.

Today, you may be experiencing life's torrential rain, family hurricanes, and health earthquakes. However, I have a flash fact for you, and it is an excellent forecast: beautiful weather is on the horizon of your life.

In 1997, Microsoft's financial outlook was remarkably better than Apple's. Steve Jobs's Apple tree was withering and dying, with a bleak future. However, years later, it would grow tremendously, flourish, and produce iPods, iPhones, iPads, Apple Watches, and other iGadgets.

Twenty-eight years later, Apple is winning the technology race against Microsoft. In fact, Apple is winning the technology race against everyone. Apple is winning by a considerable margin, and they are not showing any sign of relinquishing their dominance.

It is never a good idea to bet against an underdog. The only time to count someone out of a race is when that person stops running. The only time one can truly count another out of a fight is when the person stops fighting and gives up. Sometimes, you may get knocked down by the issues of life, but you should always get up and try again. You might even get tripped up by your own mistakes or other people's actions. Keep getting up. Keep fighting back. Fight against your mistakes. Fight against your past and the negative things others say about you.

Rise from the weight of scars, of hurt, disappointment, and failure, and let forgiveness be the hand that lifts you. Run boldly toward your dreams. If the wounds are too deep for running, then walk. If walking feels impossible, then crawl. Whatever you do, do not stop. Keep moving. Keep reaching. Keep believing.

Rest only to gather strength, but never to surrender. You are not traveling this path alone. Your family and friends are learning perseverance from your steps. You benefit all in your space. You are encouraging those who may never admit it. Find courage in your resilience. Your friends seek inspiration in your determination. The world is watching. Even strangers are looking to you as proof that obstacles can be overcome. Doubt may try to whisper its lies, but you can rise above it. You are stronger than the voices that say you cannot. Let them see your grit. Let them witness your resolve. Most importantly, prove it to yourself.

Attaining a doctorate from an accredited and reputable university while working full-time and raising a family is difficult. I need to make that clear because all doctorates are not created equal. Anyway, during my studies, I felt like my brain was being ripped apart several times. My PhD journey was mentally and emotionally challenging.

There were nights when Sleep came knocking, soft-footed and persuasive, whispering promises of rest I could almost taste. But I had thoughts to chase, papers to wrestle down. So I'd say, "Not now, Sleep. We can't be together tonight." Still, Sleep lingered, smug and stubborn. That's when I'd plant my feet and declare, "You are not the boss of me." And just like that, Sleep would retreat, grumbling into the shadows, leaving me with my purpose, and a flickering desk lamp for company. Of course, it didn't always work. Some nights, Sleep won—and I woke up with my face in the middle of page three.

One of the greatest allies in my doctoral journey wasn't a book or a theory, it was a two-word phrase from my statistics professor, Dr. Martha Hollis. I'll close this strategy with that phrase; in the hope it will lift you through moments when quitting feels tempting and the path forward seems impossible. Over and over, Dr. Hollis would say and write to us these two powerful words: "keep going." Because more often than not, persistence is what turns the impossible into reality.

STRATEGY 3 TAKEAWAYS

Saul and the Men in the Army	Steve Jobs and Teenager David
Embraced doubt	Dispelled doubt
Gave in to hopelessness	Chose optimism
Froze in fear	Ignited courage

YOUR TURN TO REFLECT AND ACT

1. How will you silence self-doubt and reject the voices that try to define you?

2. What will you focus on to stay optimistic when challenges arise?

3. What bold steps will help you choose courage—even when fear feels easier?

Signature: _____ Today's date: _____

THE POSSIBLE-IMPOSSIBLE

Unlock the Potential Hidden Within the Impossible

For by thee I have run through a troop; and
by my God have I leaped over a wall.
DAVID

Impossibilities are children of self-doubt. Self-doubt has derailed the journey of many dreamers. Note that I implied self-doubt does not derail dreams, but that it derails the dreamers' path to achieving those dreams. People often abandon following their dreams and accomplishing their goals because they embrace self-doubt. They may doubt that their dreams or goals are attainable. They do not envision succeeding and will even talk themselves out of succeeding. This usually happens after a few mishaps or difficulties, or if the road to their dreams seems too long.

Even if a goal is achievable, a person's excitement and enthusiasm for that goal can be dampened if they cannot efficiently navigate the path to the goal. This is true for just about any goal. For instance, it is possible to drive from New York to Florida. However, the long journey will become unbearable if the driver does not have accurate directions or proper rest. This might lead to self-doubt, the driver giving up, and never reaching Florida.

Do you have the correct directions to your dreams? Are you prepared and willing to journey on despite potholes along the way? You may be unprepared if you contemplate giving up on your goals and dreams.

Are you trying to get to Florida from New York, but due to a faulty GPS, you are unaware of it, and thus are headed to Las Vegas? Could your self-doubt be a byproduct of your being on the wrong path? What is the real source of your self-doubt? When you locate the source, you can manage it effectively.

One of the main differences between achievers and success-challenged individuals is the ability to manage self-doubt. This is done mentally. Put your self-doubt on trial for threatening your bright future and achievable goals. Cross-examine it thoroughly. Look for evidence that it has robbed you and others of your achievements. Look at the reasons you dislike it, knowing it only wants to harm your future. Once you are sure of its guilt, pass judgment and sentence it to life away from you without any chance of parole. Steve Jobs won his case against self-doubt. He knew its guilt and gave it a life sentence.

Steve Jobs defeated Apple's rivals and transformed many industries by conquering and banishing self-doubt. He refused to give self-doubt any space because he understood it was counterproductive. He knew that if he let self-doubt win, Apple would never reach new heights of innovation. This is clearly shown in the design of the iPhone. Specifically, the unique glass on the original iPhone was created because Steve Jobs made self-doubt his enemy. He saw the impossible as possible and had the extraordinary ability to inspire others to do what they believed was impossible, even experts who were more knowledgeable than he was. He also made everyone realize that self-doubt should not be tolerated, that accepting it was not an option if innovation was to grow.

THE IPHONE GLASS: IMPOSSIBLE IS NOTHING

According to Walter Isaacson, the original iPhone was planned to have a plastic screen like the iPod.[61] However, that plan changed when Steve Jobs wanted a glass screen. According to Isaacson, Jobs believed a glass screen would enhance the iPhone's elegance and make it feel real. The issue was that no such glass was available to fit Jobs's iPhone criteria.

The type of glass Steve Jobs wanted for the iPhone did not exist. According to Isaacson, Jobs met with a top glass manufacturer named Wendell Weeks of Corning Glass in New York and explained the type of glass he wanted. Mr. Weeks informed Mr. Jobs that the kind of glass he wanted would be impossible. Isaacson wrote that Steve Jobs told glass expert Wendell Weeks, who had been making glass for decades, that it could be done, even though Jobs had no experience producing glass or understanding the challenges involved.

CONCEIVE THE POSSIBLE

As Isaacson recounts, Jobs challenged Weeks to *conceive the possible*. Just because the glass hadn't been made before, Jobs argued, didn't mean it couldn't be made. Jobs insisted Weeks could do it if he mentally embraced possibility and rejected the impossible mindset. It wasn't stubbornness, it was vision, unyielding in the face of resistance.

---

61. Isaacson, Steve Jobs, 471–472.

Six months later, Mr. Weeks produced the glass. What had once seemed impossible became reality. Jobs's conviction didn't just bend expectations, it reshaped an entire industry.

To achieve your personal or professional goals, you must eliminate self-doubt in yourself and those around you.

If you own an iPhone, now is an opportune moment to touch the screen and say, "*Impossible is a word not found in my vocabulary.*"

To achieve your personal or professional goals, you must eliminate self-doubt in yourself and those around you. Confidence fuels progress, while doubt holds it back. What made Steve Jobs believe such a glass was possible, despite the glass expert's disagreement? I suggest there are two answers:

1. Jobs felt that the fact that he could envision and articulate the specifications of the glass meant that it could be manufactured.

2. He wanted the glass so badly that *no* was not an answer he would accept. Steve Jobs did not doubt his vision of getting a unique glass for the iPhone.

As a result, he convinced Mr. Weeks, who had been making glass for years, that he could do the impossible.

Self-doubt, impossible, and *cannot* are BFFs—best failure friends. Conversely, *faith, focus,* and *substantial effort* are the sides of the equilateral triangle of possibilities.

The glass experience with Steve Jobs undoubtedly elevated Corning and its CEO to a new level of creativity and possibilities. Self-doubt was no longer welcomed at Corning. Twenty years after the impossible-to-possible glass encounter with Steve Jobs, Wendell Weeks was still Corning's CEO in 2025.[62]

The company is doing exceptionally well—in fact, it is flourishing. Yahoo Finance reported on April 18, 2017, that Verizon, the world's largest wireless carrier, committed to purchasing at least $1.05 billion in optical fiber from Corning to fuel its 5G network.[63]

CHANGE IMPOSSIBLE TO POSSIBLE

One reason Corning and its CEO, Wendell Weeks, have soared to new heights was the lesson from Steve Jobs: anything is possible when you can mentally envision it and erase self-doubt.

Corning Glass' revenues have skyrocketed since the impossible became possible. In 2025, Corning reported a record fourth-quarter 2024 revenue of $3.9 billion.[64] Another 2025 report noted that the company was building a $900 million facility in Michigan, which would create over 1,000 jobs.[65] Corning is profitable because its CEO learned a valuable lesson: never employ self-doubt. Instead, find the possibility in impossibility.

My oldest son, David, shared that the most challenging part of becoming a US Marine was passing The Crucible during basic training.

---

62. Corning Incorporated, "Wendell P. Weeks," accessed April 7, 2025, https://www.corning.com/worldwide/en/about-us/company-profile/our-leadership/wendell-p--weeks.html.

63. Anjali Athavaley, "Verizon, Corning Agree to $1.05 Billion Fiber Deal," *Yahoo Finance*, April 4, 2017, https://finance.yahoo.com/news/verizon-corning-agree-1-05-161249110.html.

64. Yahoo Finance, "Corning Inc (GLW) Q4 2024 Earnings Call Highlights," *Yahoo Finance*, February 1, 2025, https://finance.yahoo.com/news/corning-inc-glw-q4-2024-071547483.html.

65. Jeff Smith, "Corning Inc. Building New $900 Million Solar Facility in Michigan Updates," *The Leader*, February 14, 2025, https://www.the-leader.com/story/news/local/2025/02/14/corning-inc-building-new-900-million-solar-facility-in-michigan-updates/78454504007/.

It is a grueling 54-hour gauntlet that pushes the Marine trainee to mental and physical limits. The Crucible is done without much sleep and food.[66] David shared that the only way he could pass was to defeat self-doubt.

If you are to skillfully navigate the roads of success, achievement, and greatness, you must leave self-doubt behind. Open the door to your mind and kick self-doubt goodbye. This is the method Goliath-killer David employed. In fact, David blew self-doubt to pieces with the dynamite of self-confidence and faith in his God.

DAVID HAS NO DOUBT HE WILL KILL GOLIATH, AND HE MAKES THE ARMY CHIEF BELIEVE

David is perspiring in self-confidence as he stands before Saul, while everyone else (including Saul) is freezing in fear. David did not know the term "self-doubt" existed. This creates the audience with Saul, even though David has no appointment.

Your confidence will blow open the door to your success.

To put it differently, inexperience mixed with self-confidence can create massive opportunities for you.

Saul looks at his soldiers, wondering if they are playing some silly game with him. Why would they take this kid to him? Saul does a triple visual of the young man and tries to read him, but there is not much to read. What he sees is a pageless book without a cover.

The boy was either mentally challenged or working for the giant and the Philistines. Maybe David was an undercover Philistine agent. Yes, this had to be a trick, Saul initially thought. But then, no, the boy did not fit the profile of a trickster. Moreover, three of his brothers

---

66. United States Marine Corps, "Recruit Training," accessed April 7, 2025, https://www.marines.com/become-a-marine/process-to-join/recruit-training.html.

were Israelites soldiers. While Saul is mentally deliberating, David abruptly ends the deliberation by emphatically declaring he will fight the giant. Saul is again stunned by the youngster's courage and self-confidence, but immediately tells him he has no chance against the giant.

SAUL USES GOLIATH'S PAST TO ATTEMPT TO STOP DAVID'S FUTURE

You can't fight him! You're just a kid, and he's been a warrior since he was a kid, Saul says, his voice edged with frustration.[67] Saul attempts to use Goliath's past to determine David's success possibilities. Have you ever used your past against you? Do you permit people to use your past to disqualify you from achieving your dreams? Are you using your past against you now? Are you using your past as an excuse not to return to school, not to start a YouTube channel, not to write a book, or not to love again?

DO NOT LET YOUR PAST HINDER YOUR SUCCESS

David uses his past to convince Saul that he can fight and kill Goliath. Yes, as incredulous as it sounds, what David tells Saul next convinces Saul to allow him to fight the giant Goliath. David tells Saul he is also a killer. Saul is surprised, and this news piques his interest. Who was this kid, he silently wondered. Moreover, whom had he killed? The army captain looks closer at David, who exhibits great confidence but is incapable of being a suitable match for the giant. The boy does not look like a killer and is certainly not built like one, so Saul cautiously asks David about his exploits, doubting there would be much significance attached to it.

---

67. *KJV*, 1 Samuel 17:33

David steps forward, with eyes fixed on Saul's eyes, and tells the army chief that one time a lion came and snatched one of his father's sheep, and how he ran it down, overpowered it, and rescued the lamb. And when it turned on him, he killed it with his bare hands. David shouted that the same God who delivered him then will deliver him now. He said God gave him victory over the lion, and that God will empower him to kill the giant, too.[68]

All of a sudden, Saul forgets what he said seconds earlier, telling the boy he could not succeed against the giant. Saul said, *Go fight Goliath, and God be with you.*[69] Saul could hardly believe his own ears, that he was putting his and the entire nation of Israel's future in the hands of a boy. However, he noted that David's experience with God was the best foundation for the boy to fight Goliath and win. Saul was familiar with Yahweh, the Mighty God of Israel. He remembers this same God giving him and the Israelites military a resounding victory over the Ammonites.[70] And just like that, the boy's compelling story of God helping him kill the lion suddenly changes Saul's mind.

Does it change your doubts about winning against the Goliath(s) you face?

David's faith didn't just speak, it ignited. It blazed with boldness and was baked in divine conviction. It served with such blazing certainty that Saul, once simmering in doubt, couldn't help but taste its truth. In one exchange, David scorched away every excuse, and Saul's hesitation went up in smoke.

May your faith in God obliterate all your doubts and fears about succeeding against the Goliaths you are facing.

---

68. *KJV*, 1 Samuel 17:37
69. *Ibid.*
70. *KJV*, 1 Samuel 11:11

The massive faith and self-confidence Saul saw in the boy were much more than his confidence in his men and himself.

David's resume is extremely short; he certainly does not possess the military experience Saul and the soldiers have. His resume pales in comparison to the countless men Goliath had slain. Realistically, David is not qualified to fight Goliath. Apparently, his one successful experience with killing the lion and safely retrieving the sheep demolished Saul's wall of doubt in David's ability to defeat the giant. The confidence with which he speaks, the unwavering belief he could pull it off with God's help, gives Saul hope. *Do you believe God can empower you to destroy the Goliaths you face?*

Goliath terrified Israel and other nations for many years. This continued because CEO Saul only sought the best and the most skilled fighter. He believed he needed the most physically qualified challenger to defeat Goliath. He was so wrong.

WHO SHOULD YOU HIRE TO BRING YOUR ORGANIZATION TO THE NEXT LEVEL?

If you are an organizational leader or HR manager, consider the following questions: What if Saul had not given David, who seemed unqualified, the opportunity for the job? What if Saul failed to see beyond David's youth and inexperience? What if David's experience of killing the lion did not convince Saul to let the boy fight Goliath? Saul's "business" was stagnant before David appeared on the scene, its future was dim. Nothing was working for Saul and his men. On the one hand, Saul was a poor leader. On the other hand, he was a genius at recognizing rare talent when he encountered it.

We must never dismiss a person because of what they lack or what they were born into, be it age, status, color, gender, ability, education, or belief. Greatness often grows in overlooked soil.

Do not refuse to hire someone just because he or she does not meet all your self-imposed or organization's qualifications. Maybe the candidate did not attend one of the so-called top business universities, so you fail to seriously consider him or her for the job or the promotion. Do not make this mistake. Hiring the most unlikely candidate might be a brilliant move.

That candidate with less experience might be the one your company or department needs to soar. The unlikely candidate might be the one to elevate your company to the next level. Do not discount any applicant to your organization or any employee for promotion before you look for the greatness hidden in them. When you look at them objectively, you may be stunningly surprised by the gems you discover. And do not discount yourself because of any real or imagined limitations. There is greatness in you. Feed it to benefit you and your generation.

THERE IS GREATNESS IN YOU—FIND IT

The potential-for-greatness gene is part of your DNA. Before you begin to doubt my bold assertion, let us explore some facts uniquely known to you. Your DNA is unique to you. The specific architecture of your fingerprints is copyrighted to you and you only. Your voiceprint is unique to you as well. In other words, you have specific and special traits and characteristics that none of the other 8 billion humans have. There is only one of you.

Other individuals might look and even act like you, but you stand out because you are you. Now, those who know you can look at you and recognize you. If they were only shown a set of fingerprints and not your face, they could not associate your prints with your face. If you were shown a set of fingerprints from five different people, including yours, you would be unable to determine yours by just looking at the prints. You are fitted with this uniquely complex physical design, which you might not have yet fully grasped.

You are blessed with creativity that you might not have fully explored and embraced, often because it is difficult to see and recognize. Have you ever surprised yourself with an achievement? Before you respond that you have never created glass, please know I am referring to any achievement, no matter how insignificant it may seem to you.

You possess unique inner gifts and abilities that you need to develop, not just for yourself but also for others. Greatness resides at your very core. Bring it out. My second son, Aaron, wrote a motivational speech during his senior year in high school. This is the son who received the full athletic scholarship. With his permission, I am sharing it with you.

MOTIVATIONAL SPEECH
(Aaron Dawson)

There will never be a good time in your life to do a great thing. Everyone wants to achieve greatness, become a champion, win titles, and do outstanding things. But few want to put in the time to achieve them. Greatness is a lot of small things done well day after day, workout after workout, and time after time to perfect something you really want to do.

People love to make excuses, and the crazy thing is that excuses will always be there for you, but opportunities won't. What I want everyone here today to take away from my message is that if you are not willing to risk the usual, you will have to settle for the ordinary.

GREATNESS INVOLVES MORE THAN DESIGNING THE LATEST GADGET

Mother Theresa is one of the greatest humanitarians ever to walk this earth. She was not great because of any technological innovation. She was great because she unselfishly and consistently channeled her love and compassion to the destitute. She constantly fought the giants that oppressed the poor. She was committed to the well-being and comfort of disadvantaged people.

Mother Theresa did not embrace self-doubt but used her unique love for the poor to improve their lives. She was willing to do all she could to do this. Her words, *"If you can't feed a hundred, then feed just one,"* showed her willingness to be great on any level. Helping others excited and energized her.[71]

WHAT GETS YOU EXCITED AND ENERGIZED?

What are you passionate about? What do you love doing? What dreams and goals get you excited and energized? The answers to these questions are the clues to unearthing the greatness within you. You will be great at the things for which you are most passionate. Doing these things will become second nature, and you will never tire of doing them.

Your passions will destabilize self-doubt and lead you on a path to great achievements. Those who truly realize their passion and purpose will never tire of doing what they were created to do. It will be

---

71. Mother Teresa, *Mother Teresa's Golden Words*, Mother Teresa Charitable Trust, accessed June 30, 2025, https://www.motherteresacharities.org/mother-teresa-Quotes.php.

very difficult for others to discourage them and put out the fire of purpose and passion that burns in their inner being, night and day.

Did you know Michael Jordan tried out for his high school varsity basketball team and was not selected?[72] Yes, the same Michael Jordan I referenced earlier. This is difficult to believe because he seemed so natural playing basketball. His love and passion for basketball quickly erased any self-doubt he might have had. This love and passion opened the doors to achieving his basketball dreams.

Michael Jordan forged his own path, believed in himself, and did not permit anyone to deter him from his dreams and passions. After playing basketball for years, he decided to play baseball.[73] His baseball talent left much to be desired; however, he gave it his best shot. Michael Jordan is a true example of someone willing to follow his dreams no matter what the critics say. He did not achieve great success as a baseball player, but I bet he is pretty satisfied that he tried.

Are you satisfied with your efforts in life to date? Have you followed the pumping of your heart, of your passions, of your goals? Michael Jordan did and achieved greatness. Mother Teresa did and achieved greatness. You can achieve greatness as well.

YOUR EFFORTS WILL DETERMINE YOUR LEVEL OF ACHIEVEMENT (OR SATISFACTION)

According to Dictionary.com, achievers are those who start a task and finish it.[74] We are all achievers in some way, shape, or form. You

---

72. Tarik Arslan, "The Truth About Michael Jordan Being 'Cut' From His High School Team," *Oldskoolbball*, accessed June 16, 2025, https://oldskoolbball.com/michael-jordan-high-school-varsity/.

73. Patrick Rowe, "Michael Jordan Quit Basketball to Play a Completely Different Sport During the Peak of His Career," *SPORTbible*, April 9, 2023, https://www.sportbible.com/nba/michael-jordan-baseball-career-analysed-chicago-bulls-114256-20230409.

74. Dictionary.com, "Achieve," accessed April 7, 2025, https://www.dictionary.com/browse/achieve.

purchased this book intending to read it. There was no doubt in your mind you possessed the ability to read, understand, and finish it; otherwise, you would not have bought it. As soon as you began reading it, you started your goal of finishing it. When you finish reading the book, you will be an achiever because you have accomplished your goal. Please note that you must put forth effort and utilize time to read the book thoroughly.

You will need self-efficacy, time, self-confidence, and perseverance to achieve all your goals. You will likely need effort from others as well; however, since it is your goal, you must take full responsibility for your efforts and utilize your time well. Whether your goals involve reading a book, slaying the giants of smoking and drug addiction, or losing weight, know you can achieve greatness. The key is to believe in your ability to accomplish what you set your heart to do and do it. Do not allow yourself to be manipulated by excuses and procrastination.

DO NOT DOUBT YOURSELF

Losing weight, for example, is a universal goal. Almost everybody wants to or needs to shed some pounds. Regardless of your weight goal, you must believe you can lose weight before attaining it. Recently, I heard about a man who lost 234 pounds in three years. All his friends were stunned that he accomplished his weight-loss goal in only three years.

It is noteworthy that the gentleman did not surprise himself one bit. He believed he could lose weight, so he committed his energy and time to working on it. Moreover, he consistently worked hard at it. There is no secret formula for achieving your dreams. Believe in your dreams, put in the work, and let your greatness rise like the sun, bright, unstoppable, and full of fire. Let it flow even when your reservoir sounds a low-level alarm. Life is always filled with challenges, either with you or your loved ones. As such, you must always be ready to fight to achieve your goals, regardless of what life throws at you.

Believe in your dreams, put in the work,
and let your greatness rise like the sun,
bright, unstoppable, and full of fire.

OPRAH: FROM VICTIM TO VICTOR

Many individuals have experienced significant challenges. They encountered many Goliaths in their lives, yet have been victorious. They have slayed Goliaths of self-doubt, unforgiveness, despair, and the effects of rape yet have risen to the highest heights. One such person is Oprah Winfrey. She has openly shared about being raped when she was nine, sexually molested for numerous years, which led to her becoming pregnant at 14 and the death of her child.[75]

Yet, despite these unfortunate occurrences, Ms. Winfrey has become one of the world's most influential and successful people. She attributes one reason for her success to her ability to defeat self-doubt and unforgiveness and fight all the Goliaths she encounters.

SEE YOURSELF VICTORIOUS

Oprah Winfrey once declared that what people believe about themselves shapes who they become. She said, *"Create the highest, grandest*

---

75. Elizabeth Street, "Overcoming Obstacles: What Oprah Winfrey Learned From Her Childhood of Abuse," *Learning Liftoff*, January 7, 2015, https://learningliftoff.com/students/inspiration-and-life-lessons/overcoming-obstacles-what-oprah-winfrey-learned-from-her-abusive-childhood/.

vision possible for your life, because you become what you believe.[76] In other words, if you see yourself as a victim, you will feel and act like a victim. Conversely, if you believe you are victorious (even though you have been victimized), you will act victorious and rise above all the negatives that have happened to you. Steve Jobs, David, the man who lost all the weight, and Oprah were only successful because they conquered the Goliaths they encountered.

You can, as well. Assess your life, and if all your desires go as planned, then kudos. Please take the next step and mentor someone—help them reach their destiny. However, if all your stars are not yet aligned, align them by making responsible decisions. See yourself victorious.

Lisa Nichols, whom I referenced in Strategy 2, explains how she once found herself unable to afford diapers for her son while living on welfare. Yet, despite being a single mother, she refused to let her financial reality blur the vision she held for herself and her child. That vision drove her to take bold steps—attending financial conferences, saving whatever she could, and investing in a dream she couldn't yet fully define.[77] She is now one of the few African American women to own a publicly traded company. [78]

How did she accomplish such success?

She saw herself as a winner, even when she seemed to be in an unwinnable situation. Then, she took action that seemed unorthodox or unpopular. Sometimes, success is only found when we break

76. Oprah Winfrey and Janet Lowe, *Oprah Winfrey Speaks: Insight from the World's Most Influential Voice* (New York: John Wiley & Sons, 1998), 183.

77. Lewis Howes, "Lisa Nichols on The Key to Abundance and Success," *The School of Greatness*, accessed June 16, 2025, https://lewishowes.com/legacy/lisa-nichols/.

78. Bryan Liquor, "How Single Mom Lisa Nichols Went From Having $12 in Her Bank Account to Millionaire CEO," *Goalcast*, March 9, 2022, https://www.goalcast.com/lisa-nichols-single-mom-became-millionaire-ceo-journey/

up the doubt foundation. If your situation and actions are not reflecting or producing anticipated results, it is time to shake things up. It is time to initiate your own disruptive plan.

STRATEGY 4 TAKEAWAYS

Saul and the Men in the Army	Steve Jobs and Teenager David
Embraced self-doubt	Managed self-doubt with intention
Saw only impossibilities	Found possibility in the impossible
Used the past as an excuse	Turned the past into fuel for success

YOUR TURN TO REFLECT AND ACT

1. What practices will help you manage doubt without being defined by it?

2. How can you begin reframing the impossible as an opportunity for growth?

3. In what ways can you eliminate excuses and reclaim authorship of your story?

Signature: _____ Today's date: _____

THE DISRUPTIVE PLAN

Disrupt the Normal and Expected

*The people who are crazy enough to think they
can change the world are the ones who do.*
STEVE JOBS

Thinking outside the box is not merely a cliché, it is the force that fuels transformation and sparks innovation. By breaking free from conventional boundaries, we open the doors to new possibilities, disrupt the status quo, and craft solutions that once seemed impossible. Real innovation emerges from the courage to envision differently, challenge the ordinary, and embrace the unknown.

The standard or required way of doing things is not always the best or most efficient way. It might work for a while under varying circumstances. To soar to new heights, one must often disrupt the norm. The norm might have worked for you or your business, but innovation, growth, and expansion begin with not being afraid to take new approaches. Disrupting the norm might appear risky, but that risk might need to be taken to achieve the unlikely. David illustrates this when he refuses to wear Saul's protective armor to fight Goliath.

DAVID DISRUPTS SAUL'S NORM

Saul arms David to fight. According to the biblical account, Saul removes his armor and places it on David. The armor was a bronze helmet and coat of mail, like a bulletproof vest.[79] Let us think about this: Saul, the army's leader, who was trained in warfare and fully equipped for battle, chose not to accept Goliath's challenge to fight. Yet, he lifts his brass helmet, heavy with status, strategy, and his own fear, and places it on David's head. I imagine it sliding awkwardly down David's brow, obscuring his vision, and distorting his stride.

David quickly realizes he can't move freely in Saul's gear. This moment highlights the contrast between man's way (armor, weapons, status) and God's way (faith, obedience, courage). David's strength didn't come from bronze or mail, it came from trusting in God.

Saul believes he's setting David up for success. In truth, he's arming him for failure. By insisting on his own norms, he unwittingly confines David to a norm he was never meant to fit. Without realizing it, Saul is scripting David's defeat before the battle even begins.

DO NOT LET OTHERS IMPRISON YOU
IN THEIR PENITENTIARY OF NORM

At first, David tries to accommodate Saul's normative thinking by allowing Saul to dress him in his gear. It is important to note that Saul dresses David. It's all Saul's idea, and as far as Saul is concerned, this is the only way David should approach Goliath. David tries to make it work. He tries walking in Saul's gear, Saul's norm, but he is uncomfortable.

Saul's armor is too big and heavy for the much smaller David. And

---

79. *KJV,* 1 Samuel 17:38

to David's credit, he readily realizes Saul's norm will not empower him to take advantage of the giant. The youngster sees that following the commander's path is a direct descent into defeat, with only one stop—violent death.

David refuses to follow Saul's usual way of doing things—and in doing so, he disrupts the king's norm. Though Saul was the one who placed the armor on him, David is the one who removes it. That reversal speaks volumes. It implies that Saul sees David's decision as reckless, even fatal. Had he agreed with David's decision, he would have likely helped him remove the gear. But he doesn't, because he can't fathom winning without conventional weapons.

> You must remove the limits of others' norms,
> or they will stifle and suffocate your success.

You must remove the limits of others' norms, or they will stifle and suffocate your success. Take their norms off your goals, dreams, and future. You need to know what will and will not work for you. Be the driver of your own dreams. Never live your life through other people's eyes. They might have a vision abnormality of which they are unaware. You have your own eyes. Use them. Nothing is wrong with getting advice and guidance from others. However, check the advice and guidance against the meter of your own passions and judgment.

David tells Saul he will not fight Goliath dressed like him. David disrupts the regular dress routine of the soldiers who had been around before he was born. Moreover, just like David, we need to fight against the usual way of thinking if we are going to achieve our wildest dreams. This is true for corporate leaders as well.

DISRUPTING NORMS FUELS INNOVATION

Innovation truly happens when our thoughts escape the *norm cycle*. In the early cellphone days, many cheered and celebrated that a phone no longer needed to be attached to a wall jack to work. This tremendous breakthrough allowed people to have electronic conversations outside their homes and not use a phone booth. As such, it became the norm to use cell phones to make and receive calls, until someone decided to disrupt the norm by adding a camera.

Yes, believe it or not, cell phones did not always have cameras. Now, almost all smartphones are equipped with front and back cameras. There is only one reason cell phones are now miniature computers. Someone took the hammer of disruption and shattered the cellphone norm walls. Hmmm, do you have norms you need to shatter? Investigate them and decide which ones need to be disrupted so you can unleash your full potential.

NOT DISRUPTING THE NORM WILL STIFLE GROWTH AND INNOVATION

The normal way of thinking and doing business has bankrupted many corporations and people's lives. In the next section, I will give examples of Apple's tremendous growth and success directly tied to Steve Jobs disrupting the norm. Before I get to that, I would like us to look at a company whose executive leadership insisted on following the norm and went bankrupt.

Kodak was once one of the world's most innovative and influential technological companies.[80] They introduced various types of cameras to the world, and consumers were thrilled with the prospect of

---

80. "History | Kodak," *Kodak*, accessed June 16, 2025, https://www.kodak.com/en/company/page/history/

snapping pictures and printing them. If you have black-and-white pictures of your parents or grandparents, those photos were likely taken with a Kodak camera. Kodak ruled the photography world for many decades.

In the 1980s, Kodak dominated almost 70 percent of the profitable U.S. film market. The company's profit margins on film approached 70 percent, supported by a vast distribution network and one of the most powerful brands globally[81].

Specifically, in 1981, the company's revenue skyrocketed to $10 billion, with 12,000 employees.[82]

Unfortunately, on January 19, 2012, after over 100 years in business, the company filed for bankruptcy.[83] Do you know the reason, or would you like to guess it?

The company's leaders refused to disrupt their standard business model.

EMBRACE DISRUPTING THE NORM

Photographic films cemented Kodak's main business model. This was their norm, making them dominant in the photographic film industry. Kodak made a ton of money selling films. However, when company executives failed to disrupt their business model, Kodak was on a one-way highway to doom. In a *Harvard Business Review* article, "Kodak's Downfall Wasn't About Technology," writer Scott D. Anthony lists several reasons for Kodak's downfall. The downfall

---

81. University of Cambridge, "The Rise and Fall of Kodak's Moment," *University of Cambridge*, February 27, 2012, https://www.cam.ac.uk/research/news/the-rise-and-fall-of-kodaks-moment.

82. Carmel Lobello, "The Rise and Fall of Kodak: By the Numbers," *The Week*, January 11, 2015, accessed April 7, 2025, https://theweek.com/articles/481308/rise-fall-kodak-by-numbers.

83. In re Eastman Kodak Co., Case No. 12-10202 (ALG), United States Bankruptcy Court for the Southern District of New York, June 28, 2012

did not stem from a lack of technological foresight, but from leadership's failure to disrupt entrenched norms and adapt to the digital future. By the time they fully recognized that digital photos were overtaking print, it was too late to pivot effectively.[84]

They had orchestrated their own death. Company executives believed their usual way of doing business did not need to be changed. The complete opposite is true for Steve Jobs and other Apple leaders. Steve Jobs constantly disrupted the norm.

STEVE JOBS DISRUPTS
BLACKBERRY'S NORM WITH THE IPHONE

The Research in Motion (RIM) Blackberry smartphone was once the most popular smartphone in the world. In 2008, RIM's sales and profits doubled. The company reported annual revenue of approximately $6 billion and boasted $1.3 billion in net income.[85]

BlackBerry phones ruled the smartphone market. People loved their BlackBerry phones. Nothing could be better, or so they thought.

BlackBerry phones were compact and had a small screen and a small keyboard below the screen. Maybe you, your parents, or your grandparents owned one. Those who owned a BlackBerry seemed to glide with elegance and confidence, knowing their BlackBerry was attached to their person.

A BlackBerry phone was like a confection in motion, a walking cake frosted with the sweetest icing of mobile innovation, and

---

84. Scott D. Anthony, "Kodak's Downfall Wasn't About Technology," *Harvard Business Review*, July 15, 2016, accessed April 7, 2025, https://hbr.org/2016/07/kodaks-downfall-wasnt-about-technology.

85. Scott Moritz, "BlackBerry Maker's Sales and Profits Double," *CNNMoney*, April 2, 2008, accessed April 7, 2025, https://money.cnn.com/2008/04/02/news/companies/Research_earnings/index.htm.

everyone wanted a bite. RIM, the company behind BlackBerry, danced nonstop across the global smartphone stage, basking in the spotlight for years. They were at the height of their performance, the darling of handheld technology. But in 2006, unbeknownst to RIM, another dancer was lacing up backstage—one with no intention of sharing the spotlight.

This new contender didn't just want to join the show; it wanted to reinvent the choreography. With moves so disruptive, it would send BlackBerry stumbling off the stage, never to recover its rhythm. The dancer was Apple. And when this sleek, polished fruit stepped onto the dance floor, the audience gasped. Its elegance, grace, and boldness mesmerized the world. BlackBerry and others were soon left twirling at the fringes.

Yet behind the scenes, even within Apple's own ensemble, not everyone embraced the revolution. Some early choreographers proposed borrowing a familiar BlackBerry move, a physical keyboard, for the iPhone's debut performance. Jobs vehemently refused to follow old steps, insisting that a full touchscreen would become the new rhythm of the smartphone era.[86]

STEVE JOBS CREATES A NEW SMARTPHONE DANCE

Steve Jobs believed this bold move would redefine how people interacted with their phones. The keyboard was one of the characteristics that greatly contributed to BlackBerry's success. It is a common belief that to be successful, one should study what makes others successful and copy their strategy.

Following the BlackBerry norm was a safe idea. BlackBerry phones

---

86. Isaacson, Steve Jobs, 469.

were dominant, and consumers loved them. So, using a BlackBerry-type keyboard for Apple's first smartphone was a good idea. It just wasn't the best idea. It wasn't a great idea.

In his book *Good to Great,* Jim Collins articulates, "Good is the enemy of great." He explains that the satisfaction of having a good product or company has stopped many from developing great products and growing great organizations.[87] If you and I are only satisfied with the appetite for good, our taste buds might never experience great.

This is a lesson I'm still learning. There's an upscale seafood restaurant I've loved for years. I've dined there every few months for the past two decades. And believe it or not, I've only ever ordered two seafood entrées from their vast menu, which includes far more than just seafood. It's hard to stray from those dishes because, frankly, they're delicious.

But maybe it's time for me to take a cue from Steve Jobs and his vision for the iPhone. He challenged convention, abandoned the familiar keyboard, and reimagined how we interact with technology. Likewise, maybe it's time for me to explore the rest of the menu.

What about you? Do you need to change up some of your life moves?

Steve Jobs agreed with Apple's engineers that the BlackBerry-designed keyboard was a good idea. However, good was not good enough for the Apple co-founder. When a person has great expectations for themselves (and those around them), good is never the final acceptable level. Steve Jobs wanted the Apple engineers to develop a smartphone that was great, not one that was good. He insisted on *great!*

Despite the engineers arguing for a keyboard like BlackBerry's, Steve Jobs slammed the door to their normal thoughts. According

---

87. Jim Collins, *Good to Great: Why Some Companies Make the Leap.. and Others Don't* (New York: HarperBusiness, 2001), 1.

to Isaacson, Jobs rejected their argument and told the team to break from the norm. He believed that using a BlackBerry-type keyboard would occupy too much of the iPhone's screen and limit its adaptability. In addition, Isaacson writes that Jobs envisioned a phone built around touchscreen technology. To accomplish this, they would have to disrupt BlackBerry's norm, and what millions of its users were accustomed to and loved.[88]

To achieve this, Steve Jobs demanded a touchscreen keyboard that would appear only when needed. He wanted it to disappear when users watched videos and reappear for tasks like dialing numbers or writing. This vision wouldn't have been possible had Apple conformed to the culture of rigid keyboards. Isaacson explains that Jobs spent six months working with Apple engineers to perfect the touchscreen display. He succeeded. Not only did he disrupt BlackBerry's norm and replace it with a new one, he introduced others as well.[89]

APPLE ADDS TO THEIR NEW NORM

Steve Jobs introduced the iPhone to the world in January 2007 at the Macworld conference in San Francisco. His first words were, *"This is a day I've been looking forward to for two and a half years."* He continued, *"Every once in a while, a revolutionary product comes along that changes everything."*[90] The suspense that had gripped Apple enthusiasts and others for months reached its boiling point. Excitement and anticipation buzzed around the room like a swarm of bees departing a honeycomb.

---

88. Isaacson, *Steve Jobs*, 469.

89. *Ibid.*, 468

90. Pangambam, P. *Steve Jobs, iPhone 2007 Presentation, Macworld Conference, San Francisco, CA, January 9, 2007.* Singju Post. Accessed June 12, 2025. Steve Jobs iPhone 2007 Presentation (Full Transcript)

The iPhone was unlike anything the public had seen before—an iPod, a computer, and a cell phone all in one. Apple created a new norm and built a device to revolutionize the smartphone market. This device also marked the beginning of the end of BlackBerry's dominance. By the time Steve Jobs finished his iPhone presentation, it was evident that a disruptive norm was present. A new norm had dawned upon the smartphone horizon. There was a new dancer on the global smartphone dance floor. Immediately, panic took place at BlackBerry's maker, Research In Motion.

UNCHARTED IPHONE SUCCESS

Apple began selling iPhones several months after Steve Jobs's presentation at Macworld. The price was $500 (per phone). The iPhone went on sale in June 2007, five months after Jobs introduced it at Macworld. Apple's competitors believed the iPhone was too expensive. According to Isaacson, they believed the high $500 price tag would lead to the iPhone's demise.[91]

Apple's competitors looked at the specimen Apple created through their normal lens of thinking. As a result, that lens was clouded by their norm, distorting their vision. iPhone sales were phenomenal. Within three and a half years after Steve Jobs introduced the iPhone, Apple sold 90 million iPhones. Isaacson writes that this accounted for half of Apple's revenues. Apple made $45 billion from iPhone sales between June 2007 (when it was launched) and December 2010.[92] Six years later, CEO Tim Cook announced that Apple had sold one billion iPhones.[93]

---

91. Isaacson, Steve Jobs, 474.

92. Isaacson, Steve Jobs, n.p.

93. Apple Inc., "Apple Celebrates One Billion iPhones," *Apple Newsroom*, July 27, 2016, https://www.apple.com/newsroom/2016/07/apple-celebrates-one-billion-iphones.

Three years after the iPhone went on sale, BlackBerry's parent company, Research in Motion, saw a significant drop in stock price as the company began losing customers because of the iPhone. Another contributing factor was Google's Android phones.[94]

Apple is reaping phenomenal financial rewards because one man, Steve Jobs, mentally dismantled the smartphone norm. He went against the normal frequency of other smartphone developers and disrupted their norms. As a result, unprecedented success flows into Apple's River, while BlackBerry's huge river has been reduced to a pond.

BLACKBERRY AFTER THE IPHONE WENT ON SALE

iPhone sales captured much of BlackBerry's smartphone market share. According to the Securities and Exchange Commission (SEC), from 2007 to 2012, the first five years of iPhone sales, BlackBerry went from generating $1.9 billion in profit to losing $5.8 billion.[95]

Please let that statistic roll around in your thoughts for a few seconds. What a stunning reversal! What a stunning financial reversal of negative $7.7 billion! BlackBerry, wildly profitable before Steve Jobs disrupted their norm by launching the iPhone, was on a downward spiral. In 2013, RIM reported almost $1 billion losses in unsold inventory.[96]

This wasn't a stroke of bad luck, it was directly tied to Apple's disrupting BlackBerry's norm. It also reflected a refusal by executives at

94. Shobhit Seth, "BlackBerry: A Story of Constant Success and Failure," Investopedia, last updated March 7, 2025, https://www.investopedia.com/articles/investing/062315/blackberry-story-constant-success-failure.asp.

95. Research In Motion Limited. 2012. "Annual Information Form." *U.S. Securities and Exchange Commission*, April 9, 2012. Accessed April 7, 2025. https://www.sec.gov/Archives/edgar/data/1070235/000119312512155342/d253804dex11.htm.

96. Sam Gustin, "The Fatal Mistake That Doomed BlackBerry," TIME, September 24, 2013, https://business.time.com/2013/09/24/the-fatal-mistake-that-doomed-blackberry/.

Research In Motion, BlackBerry's parent company, to disrupt their own. Forbes documents how Apple's iPhone took sizable bites out of BlackBerry's smartphone pie, leaving them with little more than an empty plate.[97]

But what does all this have to do with you and me? How does Apple's disruption help us pursue our goals? I'm so glad we asked.

DISRUPT YOUR NORMAL WAY OF THINKING

If your usual way of thinking stifles your growth as a person and sucks energy from your dreams, it is time to make a change. For instance, if you are a student and feel you are doing great if you pass all your classes, you may need to change. You are doing well if you pass all your classes, but you might not be doing great. *Say what?* Let me explain.

You are doing great if you are a C-ability student and get all Cs. However, you are not doing great if you are an A-ability or B-ability student and get all Cs in your classes. You are not mentally growing. The following quote is widely attributed to Albert Einstein, though no definitive source confirms its origin: 'Education is not the learning of facts, but the training of the mind.'[98] I remember a student justifying his efforts by stating, "A pass is a pass." I disagreed and asked him if his passes resulted from his best efforts. He remarked he did not need to do his best; he just needed to pass.

I advised him that doing average schoolwork would usually result in average grades, and he would not realize his full potential. I urged him to always do his best in school. He argued that doing his best

---

97. Parmy Olson, "BlackBerry's Famous Last Words At 2007 iPhone Launch: 'We'll Be Fine,'" *Forbes*, May 26, 2015, https://www.forbes.com/sites/parmyolson/2015/05/26/blackberry-iphone-book.

98. This quote is widely attributed to Albert Einstein, but no definitive source confirms its origin.

did not matter as long as he passed the classes, and that getting the best potential grade did not matter to him. My next questions, however, changed his perspective.

"*Do you want the best and fastest car when you are old enough to get your license?*" I asked. "*Of course,*" he replied. "*Would you like to own the best house you can afford?*" was my next question. His eyes narrowed, his brow knitted, and his hands opened like a slowly smiling petal. "*Who would not want the best house?*" he asked incredulously.

I verbally marched on without answering: "*Do you want the hottest girl as your girlfriend?*" was my next question. He looked at me as if I were devoid of common sense. In no uncertain terms, he declared, "*Duh, no doubt.*" Knowing his mind was now picturing who he imagined to be the hottest girl in school, I landed with final thoughts on his mind's runway.

"*You do not need to have the hottest girl because any girl will be good enough for you,*" I noted. "*You do not need to ever buy the best house you can afford because any house will suit you.*" I added, "*Plan to purchase the cheapest house because, after all, as long as you own a house, that's all that matters.*" I immediately noticed he began to realize his normal way of thinking about his grades needed to be changed.

When we cling to old ways of thinking, we miss the chance to grow, stretch, and surprise ourselves.

EXPAND THE BOUNDARIES OF YOUR MIND

The usual way of thinking and doing things the same way is one of the dangerous enemies of personal growth and achievements. It is the enemy of innovation. You need to stretch and exercise your mind to grow mentally. Doing this might involve expanding your reading habits to include additional book genres. It might involve signing up for a painting class. It could be volunteering in a senior citizen's home and garnering nuggets of wisdom from the experiences of its citizens.

Those who lift weights will testify that muscle building involves stretching their muscles. Bodybuilders will tell you their muscles get bigger only when they lift heavier weights. Lifting light weights in proportion to your strength will never truly build muscles. Safely increasing your physical weight norm will generate bigger muscles. Similarly, disrupting your mental norms will increase brain muscles.

Learning and playing board games such as chess can build strong mental muscles.[99] Even taking a class on a foreign subject might stretch your mind and be extremely enjoyable. Learning to play a musical instrument is another option.

If you're not actively working to build mental muscle, you're likely not challenging your thinking norms. One powerful way to stretch your mind is by strengthening your critical thinking skills, an academic term I first encountered during my PhD journey. Since then, critical thinking has helped me disrupt my own thought patterns in meaningful ways. Writing this book has pushed that even further. Maybe you've heard the term. Maybe you haven't. So, what *is* critical thinking?

CULTIVATE CRITICAL THINKING

Critical thinking is the force that drives disruptive thinking. It empowers you to dive deep into the ocean of thoughts and discover new ideas that reshape the world. A simplified illustration might be fun. Let us picture a birthday or anniversary cake. What are some of the feelings and thoughts that come to mind? Do you feel hungry? Do you wish you could have some cake now?

---

99. 9 Benefits of Playing Chess," *Healthline*, accessed June 17, 2025, https://www.healthline.com/health/benefits-of-playing-chess.

Critical thinking is the force that
drives disruptive thinking. It empowers you
to dive deep into the ocean of thoughts and
discover new ideas that reshape the world.

Maybe you thought you didn't need the extra calories, or maybe you thought about different flavors. These are normal questions and expected thoughts to have once I mentioned cake. Nothing is wrong with these thoughts and questions.

If I had asked you to think critically about a birthday or anniversary cake, you might have had different thoughts. For example, you might wonder why cakes are popular at birthdays and anniversary parties. You might ponder why the most popular cakes are round or square and not triangular. You might even wonder who originated the name *cake* or who made the first cake. Or why a cake is called a cake and not a *bake,* for example.

Why did your questions change? The answer is that you needed to put some extra thought into it when I mentioned "critically thinking." Critical thinking stretches and exercises the brain and builds mental muscle. Let me give you a more formal definition. Francis Bacon is credited with defining critical thinking as "*a desire to seek, patience to doubt, fondness to meditate, slowness to assert, readiness to consider, carefulness to dispose and set in order...*" [100]

When I first read this definition, I immediately thought of Steve Jobs. There is no doubt he was a great critical thinker. If you are not a critical thinker, I have excellent news, you can become one. If you

---

100. Francis Bacon, *The Advancement of Learning* (1605), quoted in "The Importance of Logic and Critical Thinking," *Think Reading,* accessed June 17, 2025, https://thinkreading.commons.gc.cuny.edu/the-importance-of-logic-and-critical-thinking

are already a great critical thinker, continue to sharpen your thinking edges. Critical thinking is a learned behavior.

MAKE CRITICAL THINKING A HABIT

You can disrupt your normal way of thinking and train your mind to think critically. Learning to think critically was one of the processes that enabled me to earn a PhD. I learned several ways to develop and enhance critical thinking skills. Regardless of a person's expertise, I would no longer blindly accept their opinions and theories. I learned how to carefully listen to just about anyone, respect their opinions, and appreciate their position. However, I do not just take their word as gospel; I analyze their information, quietly assess its validity, authenticity, and applicability, and compare it to verifiably true data. This is not done to discredit them but to learn and determine whether I need to adjust my views in light of the information. The Foundation for Critical Thinking was one of the organizations used by my university professors.

The Foundation for Critical Thinking is a non-profit educational organization, as stated on its website, criticalthinking.org. It collaborates with individuals, educational institutions, businesses, and the military to enhance critical thinking skills.[101] Please note that I am not being paid to promote this organization; I mention it only because I have used its materials and found them to be extremely helpful.

Why do you need to be able to think critically? The Foundation for Critical Thinking president, Dr. Linda Elder, provided an excellent answer: "*Critical thinking is essential if we are to get to the root of*

---

101. Foundation for Critical Thinking. "About Us." *Foundation for Critical Thinking.* Accessed June 17, 2025. https://www.criticalthinking.org.

our problems and develop reasonable solutions. After all, the quality of everything we do is determined by the quality of our thinking."[102]

Do you want to get to the root of the issues that steal your sleep at night? Do you want to learn how to effectively and efficiently find and initiate solutions to your challenges? Do you need assistance in navigating the storms that seek to blow your dreams away? Are you a business leader seeking to strengthen your business model and motivate your employees? Maybe you are a frustrated parent who is ready to uproot your remaining hair. Whatever category you occupy, know you need to abandon your normal or usual way of always thinking and doing things the same way.

Bloom's Taxonomy is a framework used to elevate one's critical thinking. Named after Benjamin Bloom, the framework defines and distinguishes various levels of human cognition: Knowledge, Comprehension, Application, Analysis, Synthesis, and Evaluation. All people possess the first level, which is knowledge. However, to reach the highest level of evaluation, one must utilize critical or higher-order thinking and must be able to apply, analyze, and synthesize the possessed knowledge.[103]

Tools like Bloom's Taxonomy are widely used in education to stretch thinking beyond memorization. It helps students analyze, apply, and evaluate ideas more deeply. If you desire to rescue your business or your life from the grip of mediocrity and disrupt your usual way of thinking, applying Bloom's Taxonomy is an excellent option. Let's look at an example of how Bloom's Taxonomy can be applied to everyday challenges.

---

102. Linda Elder, "Why Critical Thinking?" *Foundation for Critical Thinking*

103. Charlotte Ruhl, "Bloom's Taxonomy of Learning," *Simply Psychology*, last updated March 11, 2025, accessed June 17, 2025, https://www.simplypsychology.org/blooms-taxonomy.html.

I explored several studies that queried people from all walks of life about their most pressing life challenges. In almost every case, the consensus was clear: money was the central issue, with many respondents revealing they lacked enough to chart their path through life efficiently.[104] This financial stress often led to mental health struggles and marital strain, a pattern that appeared across multiple studies.[105]

Now, let's look at how one might apply Bloom's Taxonomy to this common life challenge of money. The goal is to go from Level I to Level VI. The level hierarchy, associated definitions, and questions related to each level, as documented by bloomstaxonomy.org, are listed below.[106] I underlined the words *money issue* below—replace them with whatever Goliath challenge(s) you face.

- **Level I: Knowledge** – How did my money issues begin? Why did it happen?

- **Level II: Comprehension** – What type of money issues do I have? What exactly is happening?

- **Level III: Application** – What can I do (legally) to solve my money issue? What would happen if I curtailed my spending? Would it benefit me if I cut up some of my credit cards?

- **Level IV: Analysis** – How is my money issue related to my income or habits? Can I simplify my life?

104. Soomin Ryu and Lu Fan, "The Relationship Between Financial Worries and Psychological Distress Among U.S. Adults," *Journal of Family and Economic Issues* 44 (2023): 16–33, accessed June 17, 2025, https://link.springer.com/article/10.1007/s10834-022-09820-9.

105. Tasha Seiter, "Love and Money: How Financial Stress Affects Relationships," *Psychology Today*, April 20, 2025, accessed June 17, 2025, https://www.psychologytoday.com/us/blog/mindful-relationships/202503/love-and-money-how-financial-stress-affects-relationships

106. Reading Rockets, *Bloom's Taxonomy Questions*, accessed June 17, 2025, https://www.readingrockets.org/sites/default/files/2023-09/Blooms%20Taxonomy%20questions.pdf

- **Level V: Synthesis** – What changes can I make to improve/resolve my money issue?

- **Level VI: Evaluation** – What conclusion can I make about my money issue? What are the professional recommendations I can choose from to rectify my issue? Do I need to change or rearrange priorities in my life?

The above questions are just a few options you can use at each Bloom's Taxonomy level.

Let's look at how Saul might have benefited from using this approach to address his challenge—fear.

- **Level I: Knowledge** – How did my fear begin? Why did it happen?

  » Answer: I began fearing Goliath years ago. I fear him because he wins every fight.

- **Level II: Comprehension** – What type of fear do I have? What exactly is happening?

  » Answer: I fear Goliath will kill me and enslave the Israelites. Now, Goliath demands that I or one of my soldiers meet him in the valley to fight.

- **Level III: Application** – How can I banish my fear? What would happen if I did not fear? Would it benefit me if I did not fear Goliath?

  » Answer: I can banish my fear of Goliath by realizing my fear of him is just an illusion. If I did not fear, I would have the courage to fight him even though he is bigger than I am. Not fearing the giant would tremendously benefit me and my soldiers. We would not flee from him, and our morale would improve.

- **Level IV: Analysis** – How does my fear of Goliath relate to my habits? Can I simplify my life?

  » Answer: My fear of Goliath is directly related to my habit of seeing power in others but not the power in myself. I can simplify my life by believing in myself and my abilities.

- **Level V: Synthesis** – What internal changes can I make to resolve my fear of Goliath?

  » Answer: I can decide I will not fear Goliath or any other challenge I encounter. I will base this internal change on the notion that there is an opportunity in every challenge. Once I locate the opportunity in my challenges, I will seize it. No longer will I see myself as a victim but as a victor.

- **Level VI: Evaluation** – What conclusion can I make about my fear of Goliath? What are recommendations from my experience as a soldier that I can use to rectify my fear? Do I need to change or rearrange how I view Goliath?

  » Answer: My fear of Goliath is unfounded. I, too, am a soldier who has won many battles. I can apply lessons from those victories to my current fight. I can defeat Goliath if I stop comparing myself to him. I must embrace my abilities and expertise as the commander-in-chief and King of Israel.

If Saul had utilized Bloom's Taxonomy, he would likely have had a different attitude toward Goliath. This would have likely led him to cast fear aside and embrace courage.

Disrupt your thinking-norm. Add critical thinking to your mind's ingredients and multiply the taste of your successes. Always thinking inside the box will keep you comfortable and make you feel safe. However, thinking outside the box and creating new norms will expand your mind and set you up for great success. Steve Jobs did it. David did it. *You can do it, too.*

STRATEGY 5 TAKEAWAYS

Saul and the Men in the Army	Steve Jobs and Teenager David
Followed a familiar routine	Disrupted the norm with bold innovation
Limited their potential	Refused to be defined by others' limits
Neglected critically thinking	Embraced strategic, curious thought

YOUR TURN TO REFLECT AND ACT

1. What bold steps can you take to challenge your usual way of thinking?

2. How will you reject external limitations and rise to your full potential?

3. In what ways can you sharpen your critical thinking to lead with vision?

Signature: _____ Today's date: _____

THE OVERTURNED STONE

Find What Will Transform Your Life

For thou hast girded me with strength unto the battle:
thou hast subdued under me those that rose up against me.

DAVID

David disrupts Saul's expectations by removing the king's armor. Panic tightens its grip on Saul—*what was the boy thinking?* His fleeting hope vanishes as he watches David prepare for battle, unprotected. How could he let the boy fight the giant without armor? Even the towering champion stands wrapped in his massive war gear, each piece built for his enormous frame, unmatched in scale and strength. If Goliath throws his spear at David, the spear will be surprised by its easy, unobstructed path through the boy's skin, blood, and bones. David's immediate focus is not on Goliath's capabilities but on defeating him.

David looks at Saul's frightful concern for his safety and boldly responds, "*I'll be back,*" as Arnold Schwarzenegger said in *The Terminator.*[107] David exits Saul's office. His brothers are relieved to see their youngest brother leave Saul's office without armor. No doubt, Saul

---

107. *The Terminator*, directed by James Cameron (Los Angeles: Orion Pictures, 1984), film.

deposited some sense into the head of their stubborn little brother, letting him know he couldn't beat Goliath. Now, David was returning home to care for the sheep where he belonged, the brothers thought. They wrongly assume David realizes he is not fit for a soldier's responsibilities.

The other soldiers breathe an enormous sigh of relief, thinking Saul is not as crazy as they initially thought. He will not risk their lives and freedom by allowing the boy to fight and be dismembered by the murderous giant. The closer they look at the boy, the more they notice his face is heavily made up with assurance and confidence. They do not know him personally, but there is something peculiar about his face and walk.

His eyes are devoid of fear, and his walk dances with purpose, passion, and confidence. *"What the heck is going on?"* The soldiers silently wonder. Their eyes darting across the battlefield, searching for answers in a haze of fear and dust. Nevertheless, David keeps moving. He glides through the army of fear like an eagle riding the wings of a storm. He is on a journey. He is on a mission. He needs to get to the water. He needs to get what would forever silence the giant. He needs to find his stone. But first, he has to find the river. His GPS: Gut, Passion, and Strategy, pulls him toward the river.

FIND YOUR RIVER

David leaves behind the camp's fear and uncertainty and travels to the river. The time it takes him to walk to the river, as well as the terrain and the weather, remain undocumented. Regardless of these factors, David is committed to enduring the distance, the terrain, and the weather to obtain what he needs to kill the giant.

Victory required more than courage. David had to find his river and collect the stones that would shape his destiny. The reason will become clearer in a few paragraphs. There is no stopping, David.

When you're truly committed,
you don't wait for opportunity,
you create and seize it.

When you're committed, you don't wait for opportunity, you create and seize it. *Are you committed to finding your river?*

I heard your resounding yes, thank you! That's exactly what I anticipated, because deep down, I know you're ready to take the next step.

Once you locate your river, you can locate your stone. Your stone is needed to topple your giant(s). Remember, those giants may be fear, low self-esteem, procrastination, past hurts, alcoholism, and credit card debt, among others. You know what you are up against. You know the nature of your giants. And you need to know the location of your river.

If your giant is alcoholism, your river might be Alcoholics Anonymous. If your giant is drug addiction, your river might be a hospital or an institution where personnel work with drug addicts. Once you find your river, you need to locate your stone. The program that works best for you is your stone. The program that will enable you to conquer your Goliaths, your giants, is the stone you should use. Your very life could depend on the type of stone(s) you choose. Note that many different types of programs will be found in many different rivers. You are responsible for researching, finding, and choosing the best river and the correct stones for you.

CHOOSE THE CORRECT STONES

So, David finds his river. He exerts effort by putting down his shepherd's staff, bending forward, and lifting his hand. With the assistance of his eyes, he breaks the water with his hand and chooses five smooth stones. We do not know how many stones David initially picked up (it could have been nineteen), but he only chose five.

Why five? There are several theories. One suggests Goliath had four brothers, so David took one stone for each of them.[108] That's plausible. Another theory is preparation: David, ever the vigilant shepherd, knew from experience that it sometimes took more than one stone to bring down a lion or a bear. Applying critical thinking, I propose another possibility: David selected five smooth stones so he could use four to warm up while crossing back from the river, before confronting the giant.

In basketball, only one ball is used during the game. Yet before tipoff, players warm up with several. Likewise, I believe David "warmed up" with four stones, practicing his aim, engaging his muscles, and preparing to strike precisely when it mattered most. As any good shepherd-warrior would, he prepared the way he knew was best: practice, precision, and purpose. This wasn't just ritual, it was rehearsal. Those four stones were the prelude to the one that would topple the giant. Note that he went through a process of choosing the stones for his mission.[109] David didn't just pick the best stones, he chose the correct stones. Four to prepare. One to conquer.

USE MULTIPLE STONES

Let us explore a few examples of why using multiple stones is a good idea. Suppose you are facing the Goliath of unemployment. In that

---

108. "Why Did David Pick Up Five Stones When He Faced Goliath (1 Sam. 17:40)?" *BibleQ.net*, accessed June 17, 2025, https://bibleq.net/answer/2820.

109. *KJV*, 1 Samuel 17:40.

case, you need to (1) know the location of rivers (companies that are hiring) and (2) understand how to best access them using multiple stones (online application, in-person application, etc.). In addition, to give yourself the best opportunity to conquer the unemployment giant, you should submit several copies (stones) of your resume or CV to improve your chances of defeating the unemployment giant. Using multiple stones also applies here if you or someone you know is confronting a health giant.

If a prescribed medication or treatment plan does not conquer a medical goliath, quickly revisit the river (medical facility) and discuss additional stones (treatments and medication) with your health provider. Never stop fighting for your health and well-being. Never stop fighting for the health and well-being of others. You might be their David—the one to encourage and help them to fight and conquer their Goliath. Remember, David was fighting Saul and the Israelites' Goliath, not his own.

USE SMOOTH RIVER STONES

I mentioned earlier that David needed to get to the river to gather smooth stones. You may have wondered why this was important. Why couldn't David pick up five stones from the land? Why waste valuable time and energy to travel to the river? This is because stones found on land differ from those immersed in water for a long time. Stones in a river are smooth and hard, more so than stones on land.[110]

A smooth stone from the river was the best weapon David could use to fight against the giant. I would even dare say he would not have

---

110. Emma Marie, "What Makes River Stones Shine Smoothly?," *OutdoorMo*, January 19, 2025, https://outdoormo.com/what-makes-river-stones-shine-smoothly.

successfully killed Goliath if the stone he had used was not smooth and taken from the water.

Small stones found in water have unique characteristics.[111] David knew this from taking the sheep to the river daily to drink. Since he often slung stones, like many shepherds, to scare off predators, he knew that the best-shaped and textured stones for his sling came from the river. And he knew the exact spot where he would find such stones.

He needed stones that were oval (closest to being circular as possible) because these stones provided a good trajectory from his sling. River stones are naturally aerodynamic due to their smooth, rounded surfaces, shaped by years of water flow. This same principle is central to aircraft design, where minimizing air resistance ensures greater speed and control. The nose of an airplane is typically rounded or oval to reduce aerodynamic drag and allow smoother airflow—an application of the same principles that make river stones aerodynamic.[112]

David knew he needed these characteristics in a stone from experience as a shepherd. You might wonder why river stones are uniquely oval and smooth. Here is a short insight.

THE GEOLOGY BEHIND RIVER STONES

River stones get their shape and texture directly from being a mobile resident in the water. The water in the river moves, and so do the stones. As a result, these stones move several miles from their origin to their destination. Constant movement causes the stones to endure

---

111. *Ibid*

112. NASA Glenn Research Center, "Guide to Aerodynamics," *Beginners Guide to Aeronautics*, accessed June 18, 2025, https://www1.grc.nasa.gov/beginners-guide-to-aeronautics/learn-about -aerodynamics/.

several temperature changes and collisions. They collide with other objects, which causes the sharp or pointed edges to break off.[113]

In addition, the stones' movements along the riverbed will reshape them into circular or oval forms. It is like a person rubbing a piece of gum between their hands, it becomes circular or oval-shaped. Finally, the fact that river stones endure such an adventure adds to their toughness. They are incredibly solid.

David knew he needed a smooth, solid, and oval-shaped stone ideal for his sling and the kill shot. Only this type of stone, coupled with the velocity exerted from the sling, would tumble the giant. David intended to deposit the stone into Goliath's forehead and close the giant's life account. Yup, David needed a river stone. He carefully and specifically chose five. Did you know Steve Jobs needed and used stones as well?

THE APPLE STONES

For Apple to overcome the looming threat of bankruptcy, Steve Jobs's belief alone wasn't enough to save the company. Apple's future appeared extremely bleak. In fact, I've found no evidence of any other tech CEO who, after being fired, returned to rescue their company from near collapse with such success. Jobs's remarkable turnaround strategy centered on identifying and leveraging a handful of innovative products, what I call "Apple stones"—each one refined and exceptional. I'll explain this concept in more detail later.

During the twelve years Steve Jobs was away from Apple, the company released a wide array of products, including printers, cameras,

---

113. Domokos, Gábor, Douglas J. Jerolmack, András Á. Sipos, and Ákos Török. 2014. "How River Rocks Round: Resolving the Shape-Size Paradox." *PLoS ONE* 9 (2): e88657. https://doi.org/10.1371/journal.pone.0088657

and even a personal digital assistant. When Jobs returned in 1997, he found the product line bloated and directionless.[114] He quickly ordered that many of Apple's offerings be discontinued, replacing them with a focused lineup of innovations driven by his vision.[115] Jobs's turnaround centered on identifying and elevating a handful of exceptional products, what I call "Apple stones." I'll explore this metaphor in more detail shortly.

Like David, Jobs reviewed many products (stones), choosing only the few he knew would deliver success. Drawing from Jobs's actions, it's clear he believed in spending quality time creating a few exceptional products, rather than scattering effort across many mediocre ones.

According to one study, Jobs drew a four-square grid and assigned an Apple category to each grid.[116] I classify these grids as "Apple rivers." Jobs assigned products to each grid. I refer to these products as Apple stones. Two grids were for consumer desktops and portables; the other two comprised the Power Macintosh and the Power Book. Any Apple device at the time that did not fit one of those categories was discarded and no longer produced. Let's take a closer look at Jobs's actions and then briefly compare them with David's actions at the river.

STEVE JOBS'S STONES

Like David, Steve Jobs examined several products (stones) before choosing the ones that satisfied his criteria. He kept the ones that fit and discarded the ones that did not. As you recall, David examined

---

114. Isaacson, *Steve Jobs*, 336.

115. Isaacson, *Steve Jobs*, 337.

116. Case Study Inc. "Apple's Four Quadrant Product Grid." *MacWorld Expo*, January 1998. Accessed April 7, 2025. https://www.casestudyinc.com/apples-four-quadrant-product-grid/.

several stones and chose five smooth, oval shapes that met his criteria. Stones that did not fit these criteria were discarded.

It is unwise to invest energy in anything that doesn't align with your definition of success. So ask yourself: Are the things you devote time to truly leading you where you want to go?

Whether you are battling a David-like Goliath or a Bankruptcy-Goliath like Apple did, only use the stone or stones that will bring down the Goliath. Once you identify the stones, hide and protect them.

DAVID HID HIS STONES

After selecting five stones, David places them in his shepherd's bag.[117] There are three possible reasons for this: (1) He was protecting the wet stones from the sun to prevent them from drying out, (2) He had no pockets, or (3) He was deliberately hiding the stones. The last possibility seems most likely—David was concealing his strategy. If Goliath or the Philistine warriors had realized that David intended to use a stone as his weapon, the element of surprise would have been lost. David would have lost the advantage and his life.

Furthermore, Goliath had a shield bearer moving in front of him.[118] All the shield-bearer would have needed to do was to raise the shield and deflect the stone. Here again, we see David's genius plan of not taking Saul's spear. If David had a spear, the shield bearer would have raised his shield to protect the giant's head. Remember, Goliath had a coat of mail protecting his body and a helmet protecting the sides of his huge head. David needed to hide his stones, and so did Steve Jobs.

---

117. *KJV*, 1 Samuel 17:40.
118. *KJV*, 1 Samuel 17:7.

STEVE JOBS HID APPLE'S STONES

Before Steve Jobs returned to Apple, some Apple employees occasionally leaked strategic and product information to the press, according to Digital Trends writer Steven Winkelman.[119] Obviously, this placed Apple at a disadvantage. If competitors consistently gain insight into a company's strategy before execution, the company will face ongoing difficulties. The competitor would gain a phenomenal advantage. When Steve Jobs regained his position at Apple, he put a stringent plan to plug the leaks. This plan was to hide the Apple stones.

Walter Isaacson noted that Steve Jobs fostered a secretive culture at Apple—shielding new products from leaks to preserve the company's competitive edge and keep rivals guessing.[120] By tightly guarding details about Apple's developing 'stones,' Jobs ensured that competitors were left to build their own gadgets from scratch, often guessing wildly at Apple's next move. This secrecy wasn't just about control; it was strategic concealment, empowering Apple's breakthroughs to land like well-aimed stones—unexpected and unstoppable. He solidified the secret around Apple's stones.

Walter Isaacson describes Apple's design studio at 1 Infinite Loop as one of the most secretive spaces on the company's campus. Located on the first floor, the studio was heavily restricted: even high-level Apple employees needed documented permission to enter. When Isaacson was granted rare access while writing *Steve Jobs*, he noted the tinted windows, the always-locked heavy door, and a glass reception booth staffed by two trusted Apple personnel who acted as gatekeepers. Inside that studio, Apple's most guarded innovations were taking

---

119. Steven Winkelman, "Leaked Internal Memo Warns Apple Employees About Dangers of Leaking," *Digital Trends*, April 13, 2018, accessed April 7, 2025, https://www.digitaltrends.com/mobile/apple-leak-letter-2018/.

120. Isaacson, *Steve Jobs*, 345.

shape—what I refer to as "Apple stones": the iPhone, iPad, iMac, and other iGadgets that would redefine entire industries.[121]

Jobs's obsession with secrecy extended beyond locked doors. In 2011, when he learned that unauthorized repair shops had figured out how to open the iPhone 4 by removing its screws, he ordered them replaced with tamper-resistant ones. According to Isaacson, the screwdriver required to open the new screws wasn't sold commercially.[122]

Jobs also used misdirection as a strategic tool. In a 2003 interview, he publicly claimed Apple had no plans to develop a tablet. But as Isaacson reveals, Apple was already deep into designing what would become the iPad. Jobs wasn't just protecting ideas, he was safeguarding Apple's competitive advantage by keeping its "stones" hidden until the moment of impact.[123]

It is wise to hide your strategies until it's safe to reveal them. It is even wiser to conceal them when the element of surprise gives you a greater advantage.

HIDE YOUR STONES

That's why your stones, the ideas, strategies, and convictions you've labored over, must be guarded. Goliaths aren't confined to ancient battlefields or corporate boardrooms; they show up in board meetings and brainstorming sessions, in group texts and whispered doubts, on social media, and even in church. They mimic your moves, compete for your spotlight, or quietly chip away at your courage. Visionaries of every kind, creators, founders, caretakers, students, strivers, are vulnerable to theft before their ideas ever see daylight.

---

121. *Ibid.*
122. *Ibid.*, 473.
123. *Ibid.*, 491.

Sometimes, protecting your stones means keeping your vision tucked beneath your cloak until the battlefield is yours to choose. It might look like preserving your peace as you navigate betrayal, shielding your vision as you build quietly, or simply waiting until your idea is strong enough to stand. David didn't flash his stone before the battle, and Jobs didn't preview Apple's magic until it was ready to launch. In both cases, the impact followed preparation and arrived exactly on time.

If your stones aren't hidden, they may never grow into the dreams they were meant to fulfill. Like beautiful flowers or fruit-bearing trees, some of the greatest outcomes in life begin in secret. A seed must first be buried, hidden in the soil, before it can sprout. Only then can the quiet, unseen process of germination begin. But if that seed is left exposed, birds will abandon the sky to snatch it away. The same is true for vision: what isn't properly protected may be stolen before it ever takes root. Let's explore one more example of why some stones must stay hidden, so they can grow into everything they're meant to become.

Even the most influential lives began hidden—in a womb, in the dark, in quiet. You were once an embryo, concealed and protected within your mother. And if you're a mother yourself, you've carried life in that same sacred space. Hiddenness is not weakness; it's formation. Consider Moses, the Hebrew deliverer, hidden by his mother to preserve his future when Pharaoh's decree threatened his life.[124] Hiddenness saved a generation. And it still does. Because truth be told, you carry more within you, more dreams, more potential, more influence, that is hidden for now, but not forgotten.

---

124. *KJV*, Exodus 2:1–3; Hebrews 11:23

YOU WERE BORN PREGNANT

All living people are currently pregnant. You are pregnant right now, though not necessarily with a human embryo. Whether you are a man or a woman, you were born pregnant. You were born with more than breath in your lungs, you came pregnant with potential, pulsing with dreams, desires, imagination, and a quiet creativity waiting to be delivered.

This is the reason a young child who can only crawl does not need to take art classes to master the art of coloring. If you were to give that child different colored crayons and carefully observe, you would experience great creativity. Without proper supervision, that child would use his or her innate creativity to beautifully decorate your furniture and floors' facades and even add colors to your walls.

When a woman is pregnant, as the baby develops and grows, she will literally feel the baby moving, even kicking. She knows she is hiding an active baby but does not know everything about the baby. Likewise, you know you are pregnant with potential, with dreams and ideas, as already noted. Research all you can about your dreams and ideas. Learn from others with experience in those areas to carefully and adequately nourish your dreams and ideas.

NOURISH YOUR DREAMS

You might not know all there is to know about your dreams or when they will manifest. However, like a mother, your responsibility is to hide and nourish your dreams. Some ways a mother nourishes her unborn child are to eat well, exercise, avoid alcohol consumption, and so on. In a similar fashion, the best practice for nurturing your dreams and ideas is to eat well.

Eat the Bible, autobiographies, biographies, and inspirational books (of course, I do not mean literally) to get nutrition from others with similar dreams and challenges. Exercise and stretch your brain using the techniques I mentioned about critical thinking. Then, nourish your dreams by avoiding excessive alcohol intake and any foreign substance that might prevent you from cultivating and embracing clear thoughts.

Just as a mother carefully selects what she consumes to ensure the healthy development of her child, you must be just as intentional in guarding what enters your mind and spirit. Doubt, criticism, and negativity from others can act as toxins, slowing the growth of your dreams and eroding confidence. Instead, nourish yourself with wisdom, encouragement, and persistence. Seek out those who uplift and challenge you in meaningful ways. Absorb the lessons of those who have successfully birthed their own dreams and use their journeys as inspiration.

> Your dreams are too precious to be poisoned by doubt, so feed them faith, resilience, and action.

Your dreams deserve the best possible environment to flourish, so choose your mental diet wisely. Your dreams are too precious to be poisoned by doubt, so feed them faith, resilience, and action.

Apple is wildly successful because its leaders used several stones to build the company, which they later refined. Remember, these were not just any stones; they were smooth stones. Apple keeps refining its stones through a process known as upgrading. For example, as of September 2024, Apple refined the iPhone to the iPhone 16 Pro Max and iPhone 16 Max. [125]

---

125. Apple Inc., "Apple Debuts iPhone 16 Pro and iPhone 16 Pro Max," *Apple Newsroom*, September 9, 2024, accessed June 18, 2025, https://www.apple.com/newsroom/2024/09/apple-debuts-iphone-16-pro-and-iphone-16-pro-max/

All the current and previous stones—the iPhone, Apple Watch, iMac, iPod, iTunes, and iPad—have made Apple a technological and financial powerhouse. Apple no longer makes the iPod as a stand-alone unit. They made it smoother when they incorporated it into the iPhone.[126]

Find your smooth stones in your battle against the giants that frustrate your life and success daily. Hold onto them tightly and sling them at everything threatening to steal your joy, hopes, dreams, and unravel your sanity. David's giant had a name—Goliath.

Name your Goliath and take it down.

---

126. Apple Inc., "The Spirit of the iPod Lives On," *Apple Newsroom*, May 10, 2022, accessed June 18, 2025, https://www.apple.com/newsroom/2022/05/the-spirit-of-ipod-lives-on/.

STRATEGY 6 TAKEAWAYS

Saul and the Men in the Army	Steve Jobs and Teenager David
Ignored options for victory	Explored and uncovered winning paths
Lacked a clear strategy	Discovered and protected their game plan
Didn't envision success	Fed their dreams with focused belief

YOUR TURN TO REFLECT AND ACT

1. What new paths will you explore to confront the challenges in your life?

2. How can you uncover and develop strategies to conquer your Goliaths?

3. What intentional steps will you take to nourish your dreams into reality?

Signature: _____ Today's date: _____

THE COURAGE TO CONFRONT

Confront and Conquer Your Challenges

*I am convinced that about half of what
separates the successful entrepreneurs from the
non-successful ones is pure perseverance.*
STEVE JOBS

David slides the five stones into his shepherd's bag as the cool river clings to his fingers. With his staff in hand, he leaves the water's edge behind and moves towards the war zone, not with hesitation, but with quiet resolve. He knows the outcome before the battle begins. Mind sharpened, muscles ready, he carries not just a sling, but the memory of the lion he once struck down. Goliath is not an obstacle; he's a chapter to be closed. And David—David is the final sentence.

YOU CANNOT FIGHT WHAT YOU DO NOT FACE

You cannot defeat what you refuse to acknowledge. Challenges do not disappear simply because we ignore them; they linger, growing stronger in the shadows. Just as a warrior must look their opponent in the eye before striking, you must recognize and confront your personal battles—fear, doubt, obstacles—to gain the strength needed to overcome them. The longer you avoid your giants, the greater their influence over your life. Stand firm, prepare yourself, and meet them head-on. Only then can true victory be achieved. As a shepherd, protecting his father's sheep, David was aware of this fact. And as such, he knew that to win against Goliath, he needed the courage to confront him.

Confront your challenges without hesitation, build momentum, push forward, and take the reins of victory.

Confront your challenges without hesitation, build momentum, push forward, and take the reins of victory. A guy recently shared with me that he is an alcoholic. He said he drank for years but never considered himself an alcoholic. He noted his family was very concerned about his heavy drinking habit, but he insisted he was not an alcoholic. According to him, his drinking never negatively affected his daily activities, including driving. However, one weekend, he was stopped by the police for erratic driving. He was arrested. After his arrest and release, he entered an alcohol treatment program. In his first meeting, he had to introduce himself and declare that he was an alcoholic—something he had never admitted before, publicly or privately. This act was crucial in helping him confront his addiction. He recognized it as an essential step in overcoming alcoholism, indeed, the very first step.

WHAT'S YOUR GOLIATH?

We all face Goliaths, some towering, others quiet but relentless. The real question is:

Is your courage greater than your Goliath?

Willingness is the first step toward victory. A person drowning in denial will never reach for the surface, unless someone else intervenes. Until we name the problem, we cannot fight it. This truth applies across life's toughest battles.

Take, for instance, the heartbreaking reality of a woman trapped in physical and verbal abuse. She begins to reclaim her life the moment she stops calling it love and starts calling it abuse. That brave admission becomes the key to seeking help.

It's never easy to face our Goliaths, but it's essential. Like David, we must acknowledge the threat, pick up our stones, and know we are not alone in the fight.

So I urge you: Silence the voices that echo defeat. Confront the pain that clouds your vision. Dry your tears of despair. Face your Goliaths—and expect to win.

You can win. You must. Like David, you will.

David approaches the camp with his sling, stones, shepherd's bag, and staff. Someone shouts, *"He's back."* David's head is up, his shoulders are upright, and his eyes are oblivious to the doubters around him. His eyes scan the Philistines' camp, looking for the giant who was possibly eating his ninth serving of pork.[127] Heavy tension mixed with trepidation defies gravity and hangs in the air like a low-flying hot balloon. The sun widens its gaze as electromagnetic waves sweep the fight area. The fight of the era was about to go down.

Saul gets verbal wind that the boy has reappeared. He is told David is back and is headed for the giant. Saul's feet suddenly activate, and

---

127. Alan Boyle, "3,000-Year-Old Artifacts Reveal History behind Biblical David and Goliath," *NBC News*, May 8, 2012, https://www.nbcnews.com/sciencemain/3-000-year-old-artifacts -reveal-history-behind-biblical-david-761720.

he rushes out of his tent to find David. It doesn't take him long to locate the youngster because all eyes are drawn to the boy, like a magnet. He is crazy-serious about fighting the monster Goliath.

Saul sees David and realizes there is no stopping the young man. He looks into David's eyes, and what he sees grips his vocal cords and silences his voice. Courage, determination, purpose, and confidence radiate from the young man's eyes, elevating the temperature of their very souls. Shock and disbelief seize David's three older brothers and all of Saul's army. Realization dawns: there is nothing they can do to stop young David from facing the giant.

GOLIATH SEES HIS CHALLENGER

Goliath's X feed pings as news about his fight is trending. *Of course, X did not yet exist, but writing about Goliath's X account was kind of fun.* Anyway, Goliath hears a man has accepted his challenge. His mammoth lips quake with a grin, and his blood stampedes through cable-thick veins as he waits. His huge eyes swiftly scan the valley and travel to the mountain where the Israelites are camped. Goliath squints, and dust particles flee from his eyelids. His massive face tightens as he meets his challenger's unblinking stare. *This must be a joke.*

He expected a soldier, broad, armored, worthy of the standoff. Instead, he sees a skinny lad. Bare-armed. Bare-faced. Laughable. A warrior? No. A twig. A wimp. *Or so he thought.*

This has to be a joke, he mutters. There is no way Saul would have sent this skinny little boy to fight him. He was Goliath of Gath, after all. He was the reigning war champion. He redirected big, strong men to their graves with the power of his bare hands. The force of his very breath could just about render anyone unconscious. This kid, he would not even need to fight. One sneeze would probably send him airborne. Goliath could not believe the boy approaching him was indeed his challenger.

When Goliath looks closer at David, he despises him. He feels great contempt. Expletives escape his mouth. He curses David. The giant wanted a challenger, but he got a chump. He was prepared for Saul's best, but got his worst. Goliath expected a graduate-level exam but was presented with a kindergarten test. His blood boils with anger as he looks at the boy. *This madness must end and end now,* he says to no one. He readies himself to sound a bloody and violent crescendo and end the harmony of Saul's madness. Goliath's following thunderous words leave no doubt about the grave disrespect he feels that David really intends to fight him.

GOLIATH IS TRICKED BY WHAT HE SEES

"Am I a dog that you come to fight me with sticks?" Goliath bellows.[128] He utters additional unflattering words as he unleashes verbal assaults on David. It is very interesting to note that while Goliath is dismayed by David's stature, he seems more disrespected. David does not have a spear. Goliath addresses David about his stick (staff), implying David brought a stick to a fight when he should have brought a spear. The giant expected his challenger to have a spear. As a result, he introduced his own bias to the situation, which blinded his critical thinking vision.

Goliath is so distracted by David's stick that he never considers the stick as anything but a distraction. David has no plans whatsoever to use the stick. He only brought the stick to poke holes in Goliath's

---

128. *KJV,* 1 Samuel 17:43

thinking. By the way, in the 21st century, words have replaced sticks. Others often use faltering (and unflattering) words to distract us. These words comprise songs, movies, TV, and social media advertisements. However, to see through this façade is to be a critical thinker.

GOLIATH FAILS TO USE CRITICAL THINKING SKILLS

If Goliath employed some critical thinking skills, he should have asked himself, "*What am I missing?*" He should have suspected there was more to the story than David permitted him to read. Another question Goliath should have asked himself was, "*Could the boy have another weapon?*" Knowing he had a spear, a shield, and a shield bearer, Goliath should have realized he was not seeing all there was to see. He should have known there were other factors he was not considering.

Obviously, David was not a soldier and was severely underdressed for the fight. That fact alone should have given Goliath pause. He should have immediately reassessed the situation. Goliath's major mistake was judging the boy solely based on what David made him see.

DAVID'S DISTRACTION PLOY

When Goliath saw and referred to the stick, David knew the advantage had rushed to his side of the mountain. Like a skilled magician, David distracted the giant with the stick while mentally readying his plan with the stone. I believe David waved that stick like it was the most enormous spear. He knew that not bringing a spear would have insulted and upset Goliath even more, because he had used spears to fight successfully since David's age.

In addition, Goliath and the Philistine soldiers were all dressed for battle, and Saul and all his soldiers were dressed for battle. Goliath saw that the only one not dressed like a soldier was his challenger, the boy. Not only was he not dressed like a formidable opponent, but he had no visible weapons.

Due to these reasons, and because his exploits were well known to Saul, Goliath felt his challenger would have had a spear, at the very least. Goliath's use of a spear (and his bare hands) made him extremely successful over the years. As a result, he believed any authentic challenger would also need a spear. David tricked the giant into seeing what he wanted him to see: a stick, but not what Goliath needed to see—the bag with the stones.

GOLIATH CONFIDENTLY TAKES THE BAIT

Goliath, truly feeling himself, announces the fight time is "*now.*" The time of fooling around had expired. It was time to end the madness and usher the boy into a lifetime of darkness. He beckons David to come to him, telling him in no uncertain terms that the boy is about to die. The cocky and overconfident giant goes even further. He becomes a fortune teller. "*Your body will become nourishment to the wild animals and dessert to the birds,*" Goliath screams at David.[129] Saul and the rest of the Israelite army cringe, and for some, their eyelids refuse the instruction from their brain to elevate. They can barely watch. They are further stunned; the youngster is unfazed by the giant's threats and will later issue his own.

Saul and his men have an increasingly difficult time analyzing the reason behind David's bravery. The boy is small, yet his actions are

---

129. *KJV*, 1 Samuel 17:44

tremendously big. He is inexperienced in human wars, yet he walks and speaks like the most formidable Israelite soldier ever.

David is as young as some of their sons, living at home, not old enough to even train as a soldier, much less fight. The soldiers believe he is going to die, but why is the kid willing to risk his life for them? How would they face their wives and break the news that a boy who was not a soldier fought for them and lost, so now they would all become slaves? The men suddenly formulate a plan. They think it's brilliant.

They will tell their wives they did not do anything wrong. They were just minding their own business when this freak of a man named Goliath showed up. They agreed to say the man was so huge that even the birds initiated a no-fly zone near his head.

"*He has tormented us these forty days and forty nights, and when he opens his mouth, fires surge forth as if Hell itself were gasping for air.*" Then they would ask their wives, "*Do you remember I told you about him when I joined the army 20 years ago—when we first began dating?*" Before their wives could respond, they would quickly add, "*Yes, you remember the same one, the same Goliath, the weapon of man's destruction? Yep, that's the one.*" By now, the wives' ears would be fully open to the husband's mutterings.

"*He came unannounced and issued this crazy challenge. He wanted a man to fight. In fact, he said he wanted to kill a man who was married so his wife would suffer in grief and poverty. That's the reason I did not accept the challenge, baby girl. Even Saul wouldn't fight, and you know his wife can't stand him. We let the boy fight since he has no wife and nothing to lose. Honey girl, I did not fight Goliath because of one reason and one reason only—you.*"

The wives, much smarter than their husbands, would mutter, "*Liar, liar, your armor's on fire.*" The wives would have known there was more to the story. However, while the soldiers conspired to lie to their wives, the reality of the dire situation jolted them to reality.

David moves towards the giant and tells him this fight will be the giant's last. The soldiers heard Goliath's threat, but David's response seriously arrested their thoughts. "*I am going to kill you and remove your head*," David shouts in a voice that erupts from the depths of his soul.[130] Most are stunned by the youngster's forceful and seemingly unrealistic threat, except Goliath, whose internal anger rages within and threatens to implode.

But David remains calm. He knows it is only a matter of time before his critics and doubters, including Goliath, are proven wrong. Goliath would discover he was utterly mistaken. Like David, Steve Jobs demonstrated that he could prove his critics and many doubters wrong while teaching them valuable lessons. It is never wise to bet against someone who truly believes in their ability and is determined to achieve their goals. Many thought David was foolish for believing he could and would defeat Goliath. Similarly, many believed Steve Jobs was misguided in thinking he could actually change the world.

DREAM CRAZY, THEN THINK DIFFERENT

Ten years before Apple released many of its iconic products, such as the iPhone and the iPad, Steve Jobs embraced crazy. Two months after he returned to Apple, Jobs unveiled Apple's *Think Different* campaign to an exclusive audience. And he dressed for the occasion. His attire underscored the campaign's Think Different name.[131]

---

130. *KJV*, 1 Samuel 17:46

131. Media Shower, "How Steve Jobs' 'Think Different' Speech Saved Apple," *Media Shower*, July 22, 2024, https://mediashower.com/blog/steve-jobs-1997-speech/.

Steve Jobs wore slippers, shorts, and a black, long-sleeved, collarless shirt.[132] He was dressed differently from how many expected a CEO to dress. However, this was a genius move on Jobs's part, and I believe it was deliberate. While Steve Jobs was never one to don a suit and a tie, he had just returned to a company from which he had been fired. This was likely his most important speech to date.

He was the returning CEO of a struggling company. If Apple were going to be saved, he would have to be the catalyst for change. All eyes would be fixed on him—including those of his critics, fans, financial analysts, and, most importantly, Apple's stakeholders. Nevertheless, Jobs boldly and brilliantly accentuated his Think Different Campaign with a dress-different attire.

This was a stark contrast to his grand introduction of the first Mac in 1984, when he took the stage in a tuxedo, complete with a bow tie.[133] Now, things were being done differently, and his attire showed his thinking had evolved. *Note the similarity with David, who dressed differently by not wearing Saul's armor.*

CEO Steve Jobs entered the stage, and the audience's hands erupted in *ApplePlause* (I know, I know—not yet a recognized English word) as if innovation itself had just stepped into the spotlight. He swiftly walked to a stool and sat before the eager audience. Steve Jobs was back and wasted no time nourishing the listening ears with the Think Different narrative. He declared that "…*the people who are*

---

132. Caroline Walker, "Classic Video of Steve Jobs Wearing Shorts While Presenting His New Vision for Apple," *MethodShop*, September 26, 2023, https://methodshop.com/steve-jobs-wearing-shorts/

133. Julien's Auctions, "Steve Jobs | Photo-Shoot Worn and Stage-Worn 1984 Macintosh Computer Release Bow Tie (with Book)," *Julien's Auctions*, accessed June 19, 2025, https://www.juliensauctions.com/en/items/229029/steve-jobs-photo-shoot-worn-and-stage-worn-1984-macintosh-computer-release-bow-tie-with-book

crazy enough to think they can change the world are the ones who do."[134] He was crazy enough to believe he could turn around Apple. He is credited with injecting life into the struggling company and catapulting Apple to the success it enjoys today. His belief wasn't just corporate, it was deeply personal. That same audacity, that willingness to embrace what others might dismiss as impossible, isn't reserved for tech icons alone.

Are you facing challenges in your personal or professional life that seem impossible to rectify? Maybe you have a personal aspiration you are uncomfortable sharing with others because it seems too crazy or too outlandish. Maybe you believe your window of opportunity has been closed by past failures or advancing age. If so, go ahead and smile. Behold, I bring you good tidings of great joy—real-life examples to rekindle your hope.

You are likely familiar with a fast-food franchise named Kentucky Fried Chicken or KFC. What's up with me and these food examples? Earlier, I mentioned cake, and now I'm onto chicken. But back to what my little research on KFC yielded. According to the University of Houston's Conrad N. Hilton College, KFC founder Harland Sanders' father died when he was six.[135] As a result, the boy had to learn to cook at a young age to help take care of his siblings while his mother worked long hours.

He later dropped out of school in the seventh grade and spent much of his life working various jobs—selling tires and insurance, even operating a ferry boat. Eventually, he began selling chicken. But

---

134. Joe McKendrick, "Steve Jobs: Seven Ways He Taught Us to 'Think Different,'" *ZDNET*, October 5, 2011, https://www.zdnet.com/article/steve-jobs-seven-ways-he-taught-us-to-think-different/.

135. Conrad N. Hilton College of Global Hospitality Leadership, *"Colonel Harland Sanders,"* University of Houston, accessed June 19, 2025, https://uh.edu/hilton-college/about/hospitality-industry-hall-of-honor/inductees/colonel-harland-sanders-/index.php.

when he was 65, everything unraveled: just four years after launching his chicken business, he was forced to sell his store at a loss. His only income was a $105 monthly Social Security check. Still, Harland Sanders was a passionate dreamer. He didn't let age, or rejection, stop him. In fact, he pitched his chicken recipe *1,009 times* before anyone agreed to partner with him.[136] At 75, he became both an icon and a millionaire when he sold the rights to Kentucky Fried Chicken for $2 million. [137]

Here is another example for your consideration. Walt Disney, the man behind the Disney empire, was fired from his first animation job for not being creative enough, according to Inc.com.[138] Yes, the man whose creativity developed Mickey Mouse, Minnie Mouse, and Donald Duck. He made millions of children love his characters. This is the man who was once fired for lacking imagination. Can you imagine? Today, Disney's imaginative cartoon characters are still a hit with millions of children worldwide (and adults as well).

Walt Disney did not allow his setbacks or other people's opinions to rob him of his goals, and neither should you. Go after your goals. If you do not quit, you might just leave a legacy and be able to help others.

Go after your goals, no matter how crazy and unattainable they seem, regardless of your critics. Attaining your goals and dreams will

---

136. How KFC's Colonel Sanders Failed 1009 Times," *Failure Before Success*, April 14, 2020, https://failurebeforesuccess.com/how-kfcs-colonel-sanders-failed-1009-times/. Bibliography *"How KFC's Colonel Sanders Failed 1009 Times."* Failure Before Success. April 14, 2020. https://failurebeforesuccess.com/how-kfcs-colonel-sanders-failed-1009-times/.

137. Victoria Dawson, "How Colonel Sanders Made Kentucky Fried Chicken an American Success Story," *Smithsonian Magazine*, July 6, 2015, https://www.smithsonianmag.com/smithsonian-institution/how-colonel-sanders-made-kentucky-fried-chicken-american-success-story-180955806/.

138. Geoffrey James, "21 Successful People Who Rebounded After Getting Fired," *Inc.*, October 7, 2015, https://www.inc.com/business-insider/21-successful-people-who-rebounded-after-getting-fired.html.

benefit you and likely benefit people you may never meet. Please do it for you and them by fighting and facing your Goliaths.

Those bold (or "crazy") enough to believe in and fight for their dreams—despite others' doubts—are often the very ones who achieve them and more. Had Steve Jobs not been fired from Apple, he might never have bought Pixar, become its CEO, or helped usher in some of the most groundbreaking animated films of our time. He alluded to this in the Stanford commencement speech when he stated that being fired from Apple was the most fortunate event that could have occurred for him then.[139]

As you may recall, when Jobs was fired from Apple in 1985, he felt hopeless. Yet, years later, he confidently stated that what he once considered the worst and most humiliating day in his life was one of his best. Maybe you can mentally rewind some of your life events and look at some of your worst times. I would venture to guess some of those so-called worst times were extremely beneficial to you.

Stay locked in. Stay relentless. The storms raging around you today will be the steady winds that propel you toward victory tomorrow. Fight through, and soon, the chaos must bow to your success.

Maybe now is your "worst time" as you read this book, or a family member's "worst time." But rest assured, if you refuse to give up, your sun will come up and shine brightly. It is okay to cry and mope, but do not let crying and moping become your theme song. Write

---

139. Steve Jobs, "You've Got to Find What You Love, Jobs Says," *Stanford Report*, June 14, 2005, https://news.stanford.edu/stories/2005/06/youve-got-find-love-jobs-says.

and sing songs of happiness and optimism and use the instruments of hope and expectation as you beat the drums of perseverance.

Stay locked in. Stay relentless. The storms raging around you today will be the steady winds that propel you toward victory tomorrow. Fight through, and soon, the chaos must bow to your success. Regardless of disharmony, face your music, and keep the songs of your goals and dreams alive. Hang in there, my friend, because today's storms do not define tomorrow's calm. Tune out the voices of doubt and fear. Do not let the down times prevent you from seeing your up times and future victories. Like David, believe in yourself and your success by seeing what others do not see.

STRATEGY 7 TAKEAWAYS

Saul and the Men in the Army	Steve Jobs and Teenager David
Overlooked the depth of the issue	Fully understood the challenge
Avoided confronting their issues	Faced and fought their issues head-on
Lost sight of what was possible	Believed success was within reach

YOUR TURN TO REFLECT AND ACT

1. What will you do to fully understand the challenges you're facing?

2. How will you confront those challenges with clarity and resolve?

3. What mindset and actions will lead you to real, lasting success

Signature: _____ Today's date: _____

THE INVISIBLE LOOK

See What Others Fail to See

This day will the Lord deliver thee into mine hand; and I will
smite thee, and take thine head from thee; and I will give
the carcases of the host of the Philistines this day unto the
fowls of the air, and to the wild beasts of the earth; that
all the earth may know that there is a God in Israel.

DAVID

Only David truly understands what is about to unfold. Saul and the hundreds of Israelite soldiers are blinded by fear and doubt. Goliath and the Philistines' soldiers are blinded by arrogance and confidence. Goliath's declaration makes it clear he does not foresee losing this battle. He has never lost a fight. He is the undisputed giant-weight champion of the world. He is the Goliath of Gath. He is invincible, or so he believes. He fears no man. And why should he? Because of him, the ground is laden with overwhelming evidence—men's bodies scattered beneath its surface. He delivered death to all who challenged him.

Goliath, fully confident he'll tear David's skin from his body and rearrange his bones, hurls his threats like spears. The poor boy will cease breathing before the bell is rung to begin the bout, Goliath thinks. After Goliath finishes spilling words from the huge entrance on his face, David looks into his own crystal ball. And without intimidation, hopelessness, or fear blurring his vision, he sees what only he could see. And he decides to share it with Goliath.

The giant is kind enough to share his thoughts. David thinks it would be polite if he returned the courtesy, so he does. His response is devoid of fear and firm with confidence. David's voice is like a .009 non-earthquake compared to Goliath's 9.1 magnitude voice. The giant thought David would have been scared by his thunderous threats and changed his silly mind about fighting him. He expected the non-soldier boy to flee like Saul and the army when they heard his booming voice. For this reason, Goliath remains seated, watching David with curiosity.

He does not expend any gigantic energy required to stand until he finds a worthy opponent. It is hard for him to believe the boy is serious about fighting him. Yet the boy does not run away, unlike men thrice the boy's size and weight. Goliath wonders if he truly needs to rise. Yet David's words crackle through the valley, electrifying the giant's contempt. Without realizing it, Goliath is already on his feet before David's message is fully delivered:

"Thou comest to me with a sword, and with a spear, and with a shield: but I come to thee in the name of the Lord of hosts, the God of the armies of Israel, whom thou hast defied. This day will the Lord deliver thee into mine hand; and I will smite thee, and take thine head from thee…"[140]

Goliath's ears boil over with anger. The Philistines worshipped many gods, and the God of Israel, whom the boy so boldly invokes,

140. *KJV*, 1 Samuel 17:45-46

was not one of them. *But hold up.* Did this boy just say he's going to kill me—and cut off my head?

The thought jolts him. His ears twitch. His breathing thickens. Rage floods his chest and climbs up his neck like armor warming in the sun. The battlefield sways. Both ears, too stunned to interpret, flap like fans. Even the shield bearer, seasoned and stalwart, stands frozen, staring into a future no one expected.

The boy is mad, Goliath thinks. *Completely mad.* Enough words. The time for talking is over. The boy will die.

But what Goliath cannot see, David already sees. His vision, sharpened by faith, stretches beyond the field and into the future. The giant's fall is clear to him, before the sling even spins.

Thousands of years later, another unlikely victor, Steve Jobs, would walk into his own valley. Fired from the company he co-founded. Mocked. Doubted. Reduced to a footnote. And like David, he refused to cower beneath giants. He, too, saw what others failed to see.

STEVE JOBS SAW WHAT OTHERS DID NOT SEE

Steve Jobs exemplified the power of foresight and originality. He didn't follow trends, he created them. His ability to innovate, even when others doubted him, is a lesson for anyone facing obstacles. Success isn't about competing in the same race; it's about redefining the playing field. Whether in business, personal growth, or creative pursuits, true achievement comes from seeing opportunities where others see limits.

Apple started in a garage and became the world's most profitable company because Steve Jobs saw what others failed to see.[141] "Others"

---

141. Emil Persson, "Apple: From Garage Upstart to Global Giant," *Quartr*, June 19, 2024, https://quartr.com/insights/company-research/apple-from-garage-upstart-to-global-giant.

refers to both Apple competitors and consumers. This type of blindness often led to criticism of Steve Jobs.

When others can't see what you see, they may criticize you, or even call you crazy. From their vantage point, it might look like you're off your rocker. But if you're grounded in what you know, then let their voices ricochet off you like a 99.9-mile-per-hour fastball off your bat. Don't internalize their analysis when you know they're missing your data.

STEVE JOBS HAD MANY DOUBTERS

Steve Jobs had no shortage of doubters. Critics ridiculed him, blinded by their own short-sightedness. Many had already written Apple's obituary, convinced the company wouldn't survive, let alone become the global phenomenon it is today.

But what about you? Have you ever had doubters? Maybe you have them now. Maybe, hardest of all, you're one of them.

No worries. Keep seeing what they can't.

I've had my share, too. Some friends genuinely believed I'd never earn a bachelor's degree. And honestly? I couldn't blame them. It took me 21 years to finish it. But what they didn't know, what they couldn't see, was that I already saw myself walking that stage and collecting my degree, even during the years I wasn't enrolled in school.

I saw what my doubters did not see. And in time, I re-boarded the educational train. It was not the best time because I had a family with young children by then. I also worked full-time, went to school full-time, and made just about all my sons' basketball, baseball, and football games and musical performances. Please know it is never too late for you to go back to school if that is one of your goals. If you cannot make the time to attend a traditional school, consider attending online.

Steve Jobs kept Apple on the cutting edge with innovations no competitors had even considered. He was not interested in copying his competitors' products. His mission was to create products consumers would love and need, even though they did not know they needed them. His ability to see what others failed to see made him a true visionary.

Visionaries don't just see, they perceive. They recognize possibilities where others see impossibilities. Their minds shape the future before the world realizes it needs change. The greatest breakthroughs come not from imitation, but from the courage to see what others fail to see.

The greatest breakthroughs come not from imitation
but the courage to see what others fail to see.

Steve Jobs was not interested in conducting consumer research to learn about consumer buying trends. Isaacson wrote that Jobs asserted consumers did not know the type of products they really wanted and that it was Apple's duty to show them. This statement might have sounded foolish then, but Jobs was spot on. Years before the iPhone hit the market, Jobs knew people would love it and that it would become a tremendous success.[142] How could he have successfully predicted the iPhone's success? To answer this question, we need to look at the technological culture when the iPhone was first discussed and what Jobs thought.

---

142. Steve Jobs, "Macworld 2007 Keynote Address," Apple Inc., January 9, 2007, https://www.youtube.com/watch?v=VQKMoT-6XSg.

The phenomenal success of the iPod started the ball rolling in Steve Jobs's mind about developing a cell phone. Walter Isaacson noted that Jobs knew that iPod sales accounted for almost half of Apple's revenues. He worried that Apple would be in a financial bind if something went wrong with the iPod. What could go wrong was that other companies might begin integrating music into their phones, just as he had integrated digital cameras into the iPod.[143]

Jobs utilized his critical thinking skills and began looking at the current cell phones available to consumers. He would physically inspect cell phones and note what he didn't like about them. He also determined that some of the physical features consumers thought they liked about cell phones could be dramatically improved. For instance, Isaacson reported Jobs felt cell phones were too bulky. In addition, he concluded they were really complicated. Steve Jobs then looked into the future and envisioned a thin cell phone that was extremely user-friendly. This was the conceptual idea and plan for the world's most popular cell phone, the iPhone.[144]

By understanding how the iPhone was conceptualized, we see how Steve Jobs was able to create the future. Believe it or not, we have all done what Steve Jobs did to some degree. You have and are creating your future with your actions. Ensure your actions are aligned with the future you envision for yourself. What you do today towards achieving those goals is creating your future. This is precisely what Steve Jobs did. He saw what others failed to see. You are seeing through the same lens with your goals and visions. You, too, are seeing what others do not see.

---

143. Isaacson, *Steve Jobs*, 465.
144. Isaacson, *Steve Jobs*, 466.

WHAT VISIONARIES SEE
DETERMINES THEIR IMMEDIATE ACTIONS

We are all visionaries—even if only in moments. The difference between those who reshape the world and those who don't is action. True visionaries see what others do not see and act. Other visionaries see what others do not see, yet lack the desire, conviction, and willingness to act. To some degree, most people are both. Sometimes, there are just some battles you may not consider worth fighting. That is perfectly okay. However, what is not okay is seeing what others do not see and refusing to act when taking action might make the world a better place.

TRUE VISIONARIES HATE THE STATUS QUO,
AND THEIR MINDS RUMBLE TO MAKE CHANGES

True visionaries are never satisfied with the status quo. Their dreams and goals drive them, and as such, they are never comfortable with complacency. They make things happen. Conversely, people satisfied with the status quo will never initiate a revolution. If David were satisfied with the status quo, like Saul and the army were, he would not have revolutionized Goliath's head. Steve Jobs's unwillingness to accept the cell phone's status quo design and operation led to his forever transforming the smartphone market.

STEVE JOBS REFUSES TO ACCEPT THE STATUS QUO

The bulkiness and complexity of cell phones jump-started Steve Jobs's efforts to consider a much better phone. Some recognized the same weaknesses Jobs saw, yet they had not made substantial moves to improve the phone. Alternatively, they may have been satisfied with the bulky and complicated cell phones since sales were booming. Why fix what others didn't see as broken?

While this saying is common and somewhat makes sense, such statements stifle creativity. What others saw as unbroken, Steve Jobs saw as flawed, and set out to fix it. He envisioned what competitors overlooked and acted boldly to correct it. That vision gave birth to a revolutionary product. Only after the iPhone's arrival did the world realize how inadequate earlier cell phones really were. The iPhone didn't just meet consumer needs, it uncovered problems users didn't know they had and answered questions Apple's rivals hadn't thought to ask. Because that's what true visionaries do: they perceive what others miss and move quickly to shape the future.

STEVE JOBS REVOLUTIONIZED THE TABLET PC MARKET BECAUSE OF WHAT OTHERS DID NOT SEE

Steve Jobs's visionary prowess led to the conception and creation of the iPad. In the early 2000s, several tablet computers had already entered the market. One of the earliest was Microsoft's Tablet PC, launched in 2001, a product of Bill Gates' foresight. Gates believed the future of personal computing would be pen-based, even predicting that tablets would become the dominant form of PC within five years.[145]

Years later, however, it would be this very feature that Steve Jobs would classify as broken. Acting on that vision, Microsoft released a stylus-driven device that aimed to merge the portability of paper with the power of Windows XP. While innovative in theory, the stylus and software pairing proved cumbersome in practice. According to Walter Isaacson, Steve Jobs saw the stylus not as a breakthrough,

---

145. Preston Gralla, "Microsoft Released Its First Tablet 10 Years Ago. So Why Did Apple Win with the iPad?" *Computerworld*, November 10, 2011, https://www.computerworld.com/article/1484530/microsoft-released-its-first-tablet-10-years-ago-so-why-did-apple-win-with-the-ipad.html.

but as a broken idea.[146] That insight sparked Jobs's pursuit of a simpler, more intuitive interface, ushering in the iPad and sealing the fate of Microsoft's tablet and others like it.

Isaacson noted Jobs was convinced tablet computers did not need a stylus pen. As a result, his eyes began percolating with a vision of how future tablet computers should look. Eight years later, in January 2010, Apple announced a special event, sparking intense speculation. As the world would soon discover, Jobs was preparing to unveil another game-changing product: the iPad.[147]

While much of the public saw this as yet another bold step forward, *Steve Jobs* by Walter Isaacson offers a deeper view. Jobs wasn't merely launching a new device, he was correcting what he saw as Microsoft's flawed vision of the tablet.[148] He believed tablets should be elegant, intuitive, and driven by human experience, not stylus-first engineering. The iPad, then, was more than a product. It was Jobs's answer to what others had missed, and his determination to get it right.

The rumors were plentiful; however, speculation centered on one bold possibility: Apple was preparing to release a tablet computer. Excitement surged, especially because, years earlier, Steve Jobs had publicly declared that Apple had no intention of entering the tablet market. At the time, he dismissed tablets as devices that appealed only to "rich guys with plenty of other PCs and devices already." Later, it became clear that Jobs was withholding more than he had revealed. He was hiding his stones.[149]

---

146. Isaacson, *Steve Jobs*, 490.

147. Apple Inc., "iPad Introduction – Apple Special Event (2010)," January 27, 2010, https://www.youtube.com/watch?v=OBhYxj2SvRI.

148. Isaacson, *Steve Jobs*, 490.

149. Jesus Diaz, "The Inside Story of How the iPad Got Its Iconic Design," *Gizmodo*, November 18, 2013, https://gizmodo.com/the-inside-story-of-how-the-ipad-got-its-iconic-deisgn-1463463557.

The possibility of an Apple tablet electrified Apple enthusiasts, business analysts, and the broader tech world. Anticipation surged, especially since Steve Jobs had previously dismissed the idea of a tablet PC. Now, it seemed he had been concealing his true intentions. But not everyone was thrilled. Competitors began to feel the pressure, especially as headlines swirled and speculation mounted. Apple's silence only intensified the anxiety. As the *Wharton School* later noted, Apple's head start in the tablet market created "major challenges for other companies hoping to cash in on the tablet craze."[150]

Harvard Business Review writer Roberto Verganti wrote that when Steve Jobs introduced the iPad, he displayed a slide featuring an image of God presenting the commandments. This was followed by a quote from The Wall Street Journal: "Last time there was this much excitement about a tablet, it had some commandments written on it.[151]

This statement, of course, referred to God giving Moses the Ten Commandments—etched tablets of stone, heavy with divine "Thou shalt nots."[152] But unlike Moses' tablet, which warned and restrained, the tablet Steve Jobs introduced shouted a different message: Do. Create. Explore. Connect.

It didn't just sit in your hands, it invited hands and fingers to move. Steve Jobs was now on stage. In his build-up to introducing the latest Apple device, he mentioned the popularity of laptops and smartphones. He said Apple had pondered for years about the possibility of a third product between a laptop and a smartphone. However,

---

150. Knowledge at Wharton, "Tablet Wars: Can Rivals Unseat the iPad?" *Wharton School of the University of Pennsylvania*, November 10, 2010, https://knowledge.wharton.upenn.edu/article/tablet-wars-can-rivals-unseat-the-ipad/.

151. Roberto Verganti, "Apple's Secret? It Tells Us What We Should Love," *Harvard Business Review*, January 28, 2010, https://hbr.org/2010/01/how-apple-innovates-by-telling.

152. *KJV*, Exodus 31:18.

Jobs surmised that such a new device would only be viable if it could better perform the tasks of smartphones and laptops. These tasks, he noted, included surfing the Internet, sending and receiving emails, sharing photos, watching videos, listening to music, playing games, and allowing users to read eBooks. Jobs then informed the audience that Apple had created such a device. Attendees' eyes and ears widened with anticipation. Jobs said the new device did everything better than smartphones and laptops. And to thunderous applause, Jobs noted, "…we call it the iPad."[153]

On April 5, 2010, the first day the iPad went on sale, Apple reported that 300,000 units were sold. That was just the start of great sales for the iPad. During the next 12 years, Apple reportedly sold 588.9 million iPads.[154] Wow!

Not many corporate leaders have had the vision and success Steve Jobs displayed time after time. In the biography *Becoming Steve Jobs: The Evolution of a Reckless Upstart Into A Visionary Leader*, authors Brent Schlender and Rick Tetzeli noted Steve Jobs had the ability to see what others failed to see from a very young age.[155] They concluded Jobs had this amazing knack for seeing around corners and envisioning how bits of existing ideas could come together to create something that would blow everyone else's mind.

The many innovative products Jobs produced while serving as Apple's CEO are a testament to his visionary attributes. That is great. However, as an academic, I must show you both sides of the same coin.

---

153. Steve Jobs, "iPad Introduction – Apple Special Event (2010)," Apple Inc., January 27, 2010, https://www.youtube.com/watch?v=OBhYxj2SvRI.

154. Knight, Steven. 2023. "How Many iPads Have Been Sold? (2023 Statistics)." *SellCell*, June 21, 2023. Accessed April 7, 2025. https://www.sellcell.com/blog/how-many-ipads-have-been-sold-2023-statistics/.

155. Brent Schlender and Rick Tetzeli, *Becoming Steve Jobs: The Evolution of a Reckless Upstart into a Visionary Leader* (New York: Crown Business, 2015), 13.

Steve Jobs was a gifted visionary, but not a flawless one. And that's hopeful news for anyone who assumes greatness requires perfection. Jobs's genius was undeniable, but not everything he foresaw came to pass exactly as he imagined, sometimes because of his own miscalculations.

Before the launch of the Macintosh in January 1984, he had envisioned a spectacular machine and poured himself into working with Apple's engineers to bring it to life. As Brent Schlender and Rick Tetzeli describe, the Mac received glowing reviews at first, thanks in large part to Jobs's charismatic unveiling. Yet beneath the surface, problems lingered. The Macintosh lacked power and had limited memory.[156]

So what happened? If Jobs's vision was so great, why did the product stumble? According to Schlender and Tetzeli, the problem wasn't the vision itself, it was how Jobs underestimated the machine's potential and misapplied his own insights. In short, the vision was bold, but the execution faltered.

It's a reminder that even the most revolutionary ideas are only as powerful as the actions behind them. Vision without implementation is just imagination.

This is one of the reasons some companies go bankrupt. It is not that great ideas, good ideas, or solid vision are not present. It is the failure to execute the vision properly. This was one of Goliath's issues. He saw his matchup with David as a sure win because he was so successful in all his prior fights. While Goliath's implementation was the same, he failed to account for his competitor's strategy. Oh boy, was he wrong, and he would later realize he was dead wrong.

---

156. Schlender and Tetzeli, *Becoming Steve Jobs*, 78

DO NOT PREDICT YOUR
FUTURE BASED ON YOUR PAST

Success can be a seductive teacher. If your past holds more triumphs than failures, exercise caution as you look to the future. Steve Jobs learned that lesson firsthand. Some Apple products fell short, not because the ideas were flawed, but because Jobs's past accomplishments led him to believe every product he imagined would succeed.[157]

LIKE GOLIATH, CONFIDENCE BECAME
OVERCONFIDENCE. AND IT COST HIM.

Don't let the glow of past victories blind you to the challenges ahead. At the same time, don't let past struggles eclipse what's still possible. Many people give up on themselves and their dreams because of past mistakes. But if you've ever doubted your future success because of what's behind you, it's time to let that go.

Steve Jobs's previous triumphs didn't guarantee his future ones—and your past doesn't define your potential either.

Your history may document where you've been, but it does not determine where you're going. Your future is being written—with the pen of your actions, etched across the do-not-give-up page.

Persistence is often the difference between failure and legacy. Consider famed inventor Thomas Edison. He held more than 1,600 patents, yet over 500 failed or went undeveloped. At various points in his life, between experiments, Edison might have been dismissed as a failure. But he famously said, *"I have not failed. I've just found 10,000 ways that won't work."*[158] To Edison, failure was simply discovery in disguise. He succeeded because he refused to stop trying.

157. *Ibid.*

158. Mary Bellis, "The Failed Inventions of Thomas Alva Edison," *ThoughtCo*, July 3, 2019, https://www.thoughtco.com/thomas-edison-failures-1991687.

Your past failures aren't roadblocks, they're lanterns lighting the path to clearer success. This is why the airline industry is successful. Pioneers, such as the Wright brothers, learned from their failures.[159] Had they also not learned from their mistakes and disappointments, the billion-dollar airline industry as we know it might not have been created. There are successful people from all walks of life who know their past mishaps and misfortunes do not diminish their outlook. You shouldn't either. Your future is way brighter than you can ever imagine.

> Growth isn't found in ease; it's forged in adversity. Your struggles shape the strength that fuels your success.

Look at your life; you can surely find scenarios where you have succeeded after failing. May I guess one? How about when you were a baby? No doubt you fell quite a few times while trying to walk, yet you never gave up. Since I am on a roll, how about being potty-trained? Your parents might have incorrectly thought you would never become potty-trained. But look at you now. Growth isn't found in ease; it's forged in adversity. Your struggles shape the strength that fuels your success.

If you are a parent, you certainly will experience what your parents experienced with you. You have certainly not outwalked or outgrown your persistence. This case (like many others in your life) shows that both your failures and successes have prepared you to achieve whatever you're willing to pursue.

---

159. "How Many Times Did the Wright Brothers Fail?" *Reference.com*. Last modified May 21, 2025. https://www.reference.com/history-geography/many-times-did-wright-brothers -fail-c16b1bcbf2c584e7.

Consistently work hard, and do not take anything for granted. Never rest too long in the bed of successes or failures. Doing so will sap your energy for future successes and make your success unstable. Goliath was so comfortable and relaxed in his past successes that it severely affected his ability to view and assess his smallest challenger, David.

Goliath believed his upcoming competition was like his previous ones. He seemed to think David was the weakest opponent he had ever faced. Consequently, he approached the fight poorly because he underestimated this latest challenger. Goliath assessed his future but wrongly anticipated it by relying on his past successes. Interestingly, Saul uses Goliath's past successes to attempt to convince David he is no match for the giant. After David tells the army chief he will fight Goliath, Saul tells David he cannot fight the Philistine giant and win, as he is just a young boy, while Goliath has been a warrior since his youth. No doubt, this is why neither Saul nor his soldiers believed they could fight and win against Goliath. They were wrong.

If you believe you cannot fight and win against the life issues and challenges you faced in the past or are facing in the present, you are wrong—very wrong.

This is a vital lesson for business leaders as well. Business policies and procedures that worked well in the past might not necessarily work going forward. Constantly revisit and revise strategies and goals to meet your industry's growing and changing demands.

David's prior success involved killing a lion with his bare hands. However, he didn't cling to what worked before, he adapted, choosing a stone over strength. Likewise, Steve Jobs saw possibilities where others saw limits, refusing to be defined by failure or conventional wisdom. Both recognized that success demands vision, courage, and the will to defy doubt. They didn't wait for perfect conditions, they shaped the future with what they had and dared to believe it could be enough.

STRATEGY 8 TAKEAWAYS

Saul and the Men in the Army	Steve Jobs and Teenager David
Did not see the road to success	Mapped out a way forward and pursued success
Gave up without trying	Took intentional steps towards succeeding
Resigned to past failure	Refused to use failure to doubt their future

YOUR TURN TO REFLECT AND ACT

1. What do you need to do today to rise above the challenges you're facing?

2. What deliberate actions will move you closer to your goals and desired outcomes?

3. How will you refuse to let your past cast a shadow over your future?

Signature: _____ Today's date: _____

THE WAY TO WALK IS RUN

Take Actionable Steps to Achieve Your Success

Don't let the voice of others' opinions
drown out your own inner voice.
STEVE JOBS

Goliath's massive frame is now in the upright position. His muscular neck displays his huge head like an oversized trophy. His face contorts with anger. He is still seething that Saul would publicly disrespect him by sending a boy to fight him. With his shield-bearer leading the way, Goliath begins the slow, laborious walk as his massive feet crush and splatter the dust beneath. His mouth salivates in anticipation of dismembering his challenger. This would be his easiest victory yet. It would add another death notch to his belt—a small one, since the boy was one of his smallest victims. However, a win is a win.

Walking towards the boy would certainly require more energy than ripping the youngster's body apart from its skinny frame.

David decides to help Goliath. He would save some of the giant's energy by shortening the distance for the big man. What David does next doesn't speak—it roars. He does what no one is expecting. He runs towards Goliath. [160]

DAVID RUNS TOWARDS GOLIATH

David is not a trained soldier, yet his steps march with the resolve of one. He exposes Saul and his soldiers, revealing what passion looks like when it confronts fear. For Saul and his men, fighting the enemy is just a job. But to David, it's personal. While they retreat, he charges forward. While they avoid the problem, he confronts it head-on. Saul and his army are paralyzed by fear, hoping that ignoring Goliath will somehow make him vanish. But David knows better—courage doesn't shrink from confrontation; it runs toward it.

Giants don't disappear, they must be conquered.
Stand firm, take aim, and let courage be your stone.

Goliaths will never retreat, they exist to challenge, distract, and overpower. Their sole purpose is to cast shadows over your vision, shake your resolve, and stand between you and your destiny. But your mission is clear: face them head-on, dismantle their power, and take back control before they consume your dreams, your strength, and your future. Giants don't disappear, they must be conquered. Stand firm, take aim, and let courage be your stone. Hasten your pace to destroy whatever Goliath represents in your life. In the context of your life, Goliath is not a person per se—it is everything that seeks to destroy and kill your dreams and even take your life.

The longer you take to address Goliath, the longer it will torment

---

160. *KJV*, 1 Samuel 17:48

and stress you. Let's take a moment and look at some of Goliath of Gath's characteristics. He was tall, big, intense, and intimidating, and those who saw and heard him feared for their life—except David. Goliath made his intentions clear: he wanted to fight, defeat, enslave the Israelites, and kill David.

David knew the only way to rid Israel of Goliath was to kill him. Let me be painfully clear: if your spouse or boss happens to be named Goliath, I am *not* advocating stoning, slaying, or any Old Testament-style conflict resolution.

Victory over your personal Goliath doesn't require a physical stone, it requires wisdom, perseverance, and the courage to take the proper steps. These can include prayer, counsel, or other decisive actions. The fight is yours to win. Earlier, I mentioned there were several different Goliaths, such as procrastination, illicit drugs, and alcoholism. Gambling and verbal abuse are others. You can identify your Goliaths by looking at their intentions. Once you identify your Goliaths, take swift action like David. Your bright future depends on the actions you take now. Do not let your future down. Do not let yourself down.

About six years ago, I met a lady who faced her own scary Goliath. Like the Israelites, she was doing her daily routine and going about life like everyone else. However, during a medical appointment, her doctor informed her that he needed to send her for more medical tests.

After the tests, it was determined she had stage four cancer. Initially, she was in shock and disbelief, which turned into sadness and depression. She stated all these were compounded because she had not done her yearly mammogram.

She blamed herself. However, now, she realized she needed to make an important decision. Either she would continue in depression and fear, or she would face and fight cancer.

As with Saul, she realized her Goliath would not go away if she ignored it. Its goal was to destroy her body and kill her. She decided to quickly face and attack cancer by doing a lot of online research about different cancer drugs and following her doctor's advice. Recently, I saw her at church, and with a bubbling smile, she declared she was cancer-free.

Not everyone who fights Goliath-cancer becomes cancer-free. However, no one will ever beat this or any other goliath by not taking decisive action to fight. And let me add, cancer can never truly defeat the one who fights it. Former ESPN host Stuart Scott, who fought his cancerous Goliath for seven years, might have said it best: "*When you die, it does not mean that you lose to cancer. You beat cancer by how you live, why you live, and in the manner in which you live.*"[161] Well said, Sir.

David rushes to fight Goliath for the Israelites' future. Remember, it was not his fight. Some of those for whom he was fighting had criticized him and doubted him. Nevertheless, that did not faze David or diminish his decision to fight Goliath. He was going to fight.

What would you do if Goliath showed up unannounced on your doorstep or the doorstep of a loved one? Would you fight for yourself and fight for your loved one? Hopefully, you answered in the affirmative.

Fighting could mean visiting them in the hospital or sending a card. It might involve praying for them or texting words of encouragement. Some time ago, I visited the hospital to visit one of my mom's

---

161. Scott, Stuart. "When you die, it does not mean that you lose to cancer." *V Foundation*, January 4, 2015. Accessed April 7, 2025. https://www.v.org/story/when-you-die-it-does-not-mean-that-you-lose-to-cancer-stuart-scott/.

friends. I was told that some in the hospital had no visitors to support them in their fight, emotionally. My heart broke. If you have loved ones in a hospital or nursing home and can visit them, please do so. If you are facing Goliath and feeling alone, please seek help.

NOT ALL GOLIATHS ARE VISIBLE TO OTHERS

The Goliath from which Saul and the army fled and whom David fought was visible to all in the region. Those at the time knew how he looked and saw the frightening effect he had on the Israelite army. They heard the giant's rambunctious voice filled with threats and intimidation. He was an enormously large human being. Yet, the Goliaths we often encounter are not always visible to others. You could be wrestling with Goliaths this very moment, and still, your family and friends have no idea.

If this is the case, I implore you to seek help and seek it quickly. There are no Goliaths you have faced or are facing that others have not faced and conquered. There is no reason to be embarrassed or ashamed. There is no need to constantly hide behind the pictures and videos on your social media profile, forced smiles, the glamor of makeup, or the makeup of muscles and nice clothes.

Much too often, people hurt and struggle in private without warranted support. I am in no way suggesting you broadcast your business to every Tom, Dick, and Sherry. However, if the Goliaths of life are overwhelming you, please seek professional help and seek it quickly. Your health, your livelihood, your future, and the future of those you care about depend on your decision to expose and confront your life-threatening Goliath(s).

Israel's future as an independent nation depended on whether there was a man who would fight and kill Goliath. During that time, women were not allowed to fight in the army. David was not asked to fight Goliath. He did not even volunteer. He insisted.

His courageous actions have been retold for generations. Many have long heard about the boy who used a stone to kill the giant. What is often lost in the story is that he ran towards the giant. I will document five reasons for what David's running illustrates.

SUCCESS IS PURPOSEFUL

First, David running toward the giant shows that success is purposeful. People who want to give themselves the best opportunity to achieve their goals will be deliberate in their actions. No one told David he had to run. In fact, it might have been safer if he had walked, since the Philistines and the Israelites were on opposite mountains, with a valley between them.[162] This meant David ran down the mountain into the valley and up the mountain where the Philistines were located.

David wanted to get on his competitor's territory as quickly as possible. Since the giant was huge, David knew Goliath would not have been as agile and quick as he was. David did what he knew his competitor was not good at. He concluded that running was the best and most efficient option to quickly achieve his goal.

Running toward the giant, David was empowered to gain ground faster than his competitor could. However, running required him to expend more energy at an increased pace. This seemed risky because he needed considerable energy to confront the enormous giant. David would not have run if this had been a wrestling or MMA match because he recognized the importance of conserving his energy for the fight. Nevertheless, in his battle, all he needed was to close the

---

162. *KJV*, 1 Samuel 17:3

distance to Goliath as quickly as possible. Then, he could launch his stone before the giant or the armor bearer realized what he was doing. *Success is never accidental; it results from deliberate and calculated actions.*

If you want to be successful at anything, you must purport to be successful. You must make up your mind that no matter how huge and fearsome the Goliath you face, you will be successful. Quitting is never a good option. If David had let fear dictate his steps, the battlefield would have swallowed his dreams, and history would have never known his triumph. Victory doesn't belong to those who hesitate at the starting line, it belongs to those who charge forward, defying the odds. The race against life's challenges isn't won by standing still but by pushing ahead with unwavering determination. Every obstacle is a hurdle, every doubt a headwind, but those who endure, who refuse to slow their pace, will break through the finish line of success. Success isn't for the hesitant, it's for the relentless. Run toward your challenges and let perseverance be your victory lap.

Success isn't for the hesitant, it's for the relentless. Run toward your challenges and let perseverance be your victory lap.

Had David retreated, the entire Philistine army would have descended on the Israelites and killed them. Had he retreated, he would have lost the opportunity to win the prizes—the king's daughter as wife, riches, and his family's cessation of paying taxes. David knew that to reap the benefits of his plan, he had to be deliberate in his actions. He had to execute his plan.

Second, David running toward the giant shows he is passionate about his actions. He was not going to fight Goliath for show. David strongly feels Goliath disrespected his God, who saved him from the lion. As such, his passion fueled and energized him. Remember, he has just finished a round trip to the river. However, the energy consumed by his round trip to the river did not nullify his passion. If you are passionate about defeating your Goliath, your passion will energize you. It will ignite your fortitude and strengthen your resolve.

The Merriam-Webster dictionary defines passion as an "*intense, driving, or overmastering feeling or conviction.*"[163] David was so passionate and driven to win against Goliath that he utilized the best and fastest vehicle available: his feet. David was not at all concerned that Goliath was significantly bigger, stronger, and more experienced than he was.

He was not concerned that, despite Goliath's size, the giant had another giant walking in front of him carrying a shield. David was not dismayed that Goliath had killed many men when David had only killed a lion. He did not compare himself to Goliath. If he had, he might have been fearful, like Saul and the army. It was David's passion for success that energized his feet.

Saul and the army fled from Goliath. In their eyes, they were simply trying to do their job as best as they could. Few understood the daily burden of being soldiers. It was an extremely stressful and demanding role. They had to endure hours in the sun and were often away from their loved ones for weeks at a time.

Furthermore, the pay was inadequate, yet they continually risked their lives. They had witnessed many fellow soldiers die on the battlefield. They were tough men, and many would have empathized with their plight. Goliath was not someone to confront, *or so they thought.*

---

163. Merriam-Webster, s.v. "Passion," Merriam-Webster.com Dictionary, accessed April 7, 2025, https://www.merriam-webster.com/dictionary/passion.

Undoubtedly, Saul and his soldiers longed to rid themselves of the problem—Goliath. For nearly six weeks, the giant threatened their lives and freedom. Morning and evening, he tested both their courage and their livelihoods. Yet Saul and his men lacked passion. Without it, even purpose turns into obligation, what they did became just a job. But when passion is present, that job transforms into a duty. It becomes an act of service.

Leaders who are passionate about their companies and their responsibilities become better leaders. People who are passionate about what they do are better employees and employers. Those who are only concerned about paychecks become automated employees. Those passionate about serving customers and consumers should be valued and treated as such. These are the ones who do not call out sick when they are not ill. They are the ones who will go the extra mile for the customer and build a brand. They go beyond the boundaries of their pay grade.

Likewise, when you are passionate about something, doing more than is required is easy. When you are passionate about someone, trying to make them happy becomes effortless. Your passion will drive your action. Saul, the leader of the army, had a spear, armor, and war experience. David did not have any war accomplishments on his resume, but what he had was passion. As a result, he passionately took on a role that was not his own, one for which he was not qualified. David's passion empowered him to accomplish what the passionless Saul doubted he could accomplish. Sadly, what Saul lacked was passion. As such, being a soldier became a job to him, not a duty.

Third, David's running toward the giant reveals how much value he placed on time. Too much time had already been wasted. Fear had deposited inaction in Saul and the soldiers. They were busy running away in circles with no clear plan in mind. They had caused Goliath to put their lives on hold. They were living way below their potential as soldiers because they did not face and address their Goliath issue. In fact, the time and the hard work they endured in training to be soldiers were not benefiting them now. It could be viewed as wasted time as well.

It may be argued that they had the experience and the expertise to be great soldiers. However, their inaction negated their potential. It is tragic and a waste of time when someone refuses to utilize his or her qualifications because of fear.

For forty days, the soldiers fled each time Goliath rose to challenge them—forty wasted days. It was as if Israel had no army at all. They were imposters. They dressed as soldiers, wore helmets, and had spears, but were they really soldiers? You may consider this a harsh question, but is one's attire alone conclusive in determining who one really is?

Saul and his men had forty days to show Goliath and the Philistine soldiers who they really were—skilled soldiers. Yet, over the forty days, they continuously showed the Philistines that they were wannabe soldiers. It would take a shepherd boy who valued his time and punched Goliath's clock. David didn't carry the weapons of a soldier, but he bore something greater: the weapon of courage. Soon, all would witness it firsthand.

David only left his sheep with the keeper to deliver his brother's lunch. But the time spent speaking with the soldiers, his brothers, and Saul, along with his journey to the river and back, had cost him valuable time. No doubt, the keeper would have expected his return hours earlier. In addition, his father would likely be worried—*maybe*. David realized that the longer he spent conversing with Goliath, the longer it would take him to resume his daily tasks. He realized that the longer he took to attack the giant, the longer the time he was giving the giant to attack him. He needed to silence the giant now. Time was too valuable to waste.

Fourth, David's running toward the giant shows that he was determined to kill Goliath as soon as possible. He was determined to achieve his goal. He was focused on the prize. He was not going to risk anything or anyone stopping him from getting in the best position to topple the giant. Remember, his three older brothers were part of Saul's army. Undoubtedly, they wanted to stop David. They wanted to save their youngest brother's life.

Furthermore, they wanted to stop David because he was doing what they should have done. His brothers were annoyed that David was there instead of where they thought he should be, attending to the sheep.

Others, including those closest to you, may try to discourage and even stop you from reaching your goals. This is because they are either wasting time or have wasted time on their own aspirations. David knew his brothers had been squandering crucial time by not fighting Goliath. Though they were unhappy with him, he was determined to do what they had not done.

David likely feared his brothers would band together and physically stop him. His brothers were undoubtedly bigger and stronger than he was, and three were at the battle site. His oldest brother had already reprimanded him for being in the war zone. David knew this would be his only chance to prove to his brothers and Saul that he could truly kill the giant.

He didn't want to waste time fighting his brothers or Saul. If he had to, maybe he would. Goliath was the real enemy. This is who David would fight, and he wasn't willing to take any chance of anyone stopping him. Maybe it was because he was a shepherd and instinctively knew to confront an enemy as soon as he encountered one. Why would he waste valuable time fighting a bird when a lion scanned his sheep? David realized fighting the wrong battle would waste valuable time. He desperately needed to focus on the enemy at hand.

Fifth, David's running toward the giant reveals that he was running away from the fear and negativity that had infected Saul and his men. He refused to stay any longer in the company of doubt and fear. David knew if he was going to soar to new heights, he needed to leave the non-believers behind. He knew that the journey to his personal success solely rested in his hands and feet. By running towards Goliath, David beautifully displays the key characteristics of the necessary action to make one successful. It is no surprise that Steve Jobs displayed these characteristics as well.

STEVE JOBS'S RUN-ACTIONS

Steve Jobs became successful because he was purposeful. As I noted earlier, success is purposeful. It results from intentional actions. Apple's phenomenal success is not accidental. It is a result of deliberate action. Steve Jobs purposely stopped production on costly projects and streamlined Apple's focus. Furthermore, he created iTunes in 2003 and the App Store in 2008, and both have raised the bar of Apple's success.[164]

Obviously, if Steve Jobs had panicked and delayed action when Apple was in financial trouble, the company would not have survived. He did what he knew he needed to do, and he ran with it. If he had waited to implement his strategies, it would have only increased the

---

164. Luke Dormehl, "Today in Apple History: App Store Opens Its Virtual Doors," *Cult of Mac*, July 10, 2024, accessed June 20, 2025, https://www.cultofmac.com/news/apple-app-store-launch.

likelihood of Apple's ultimate failure. I am not implying Jobs's decisive actions were easy. In fact, he made some extremely difficult decisions that were not popular among Apple employees.

In 1997, Steve Jobs made arguably some of the toughest decisions to save Apple. When Jobs was fired from Apple, the company was losing substantial amounts of money. Apple lost $1 billion between September 27, 1996, and September 26, 1997.[165] Consequently, the members of Apple's board of directors at the time were determined to break up Apple and sell it. However, when Jobs returned to Apple in 1997, he compelled the majority of the board to resign, according to Isaacson.[166] He further noted that one of the board members was Mark Markkula, who invested hundreds of thousands of dollars twenty years earlier and helped Steve Jobs get Apple off the ground. Jobs understood he needed a board filled with individuals who believed Apple could survive. Steve Jobs's decisive and strategic action to oust those who wished to dismantle Apple set the company on a path to enormous success.

STEVE JOBS CREDITS HIS PASSION FOR HIS AND APPLE'S SUCCESS

Steve Jobs became successful because he was passionate about achieving his dreams. He was extremely passionate about Apple's success and the products the company provided for its customers.

In an interview with Bill Gates at the 2007 D5 Conference, Steve Jobs shared a critical truth: passion isn't optional but essential. Without deep passion, he argued, people give up when challenges arise. He knew from experience that success didn't come from ease, but

---

165. Liu, Robert. 1997. "Apple reports wider losses." *CNN*, October 15, 1997. Accessed April 7, 2025.
166. Isaacson, *Steve Jobs*, 318-319.

from enduring when things get hard. Apple's rise wasn't fueled by luck, it was built on intense purpose, focused action, and an unshakable belief in their vision.[167]

Jobs made it clear that one of the reasons for his success was his passion for what he did at Apple. This passion enabled him to make (and live with) some of the many tough decisions he made at Apple. This passion also led Apple to develop and make products that people really love and enjoy. Upon further research, it seems that Steve Jobs's real passion was not just making products people liked.

His true passion was positively changing people's lives by making great products. This is what he wanted customers to know. He said this when speaking to a group of Apple employees (this was the same occasion I mentioned earlier when he spoke wearing shorts and slippers). *"What we're about isn't making boxes for people to get their jobs done…but Apple is about something more than that. Apple at its core— its core value is that we believe that people with passion can change the world for the better. That's what we believe."*[168] I argue that when people's true passion is to help others genuinely, they will always be successful. They might even become rich like Steve Jobs did. However, those whose true passion is only to get rich will forever be poor.

Like Goliath-killer David, Steve Jobs became successful because he greatly valued time. David ran towards Goliath, and Steve Jobs ran towards perfecting Apple's products by utilizing the time—any available time. He often worked long hours and required Apple employees to do the same. One such time was when Jobs was unhappy with how

---

167. Steve Jobs, interview by Walt Mossberg and Kara Swisher, *D5: All Things Digital Conference,* May 30, 2007, AllThingsD, video, https://allthingsd.com/20070531/d5-gates-jobs-transcript/.

168. Carmine Gallo, "As Steve Jobs Once Said, People with Passion Can Change the World," *Entrepreneur,* July 8, 2015, accessed April 7, 2025, https://www.entrepreneur.com/leadership/as-steve-jobs-once-said-people-with-passion-can-change/248079.

the original iPhone looked after being worked on for nine months. According to Walter Isaacson, Jobs told his team they would be working nights and weekends, and if they desired, he could give them guns to kill others and themselves. They opted to work nights and weekends. This resulted in an iPhone that everyone was pleased with.[169]

Now, could they have accomplished this without working nights and weekends? Of course. However, what that would have done was delay them from reaching their goal of delivering a fine product to change consumer lives. Brainyquote.com quotes Steve Jobs as saying his *"favorite things in life don't cost any money; it's really clear that the most precious resource we all have is time."*[170] When people consider something precious, they value it. No one should waste time trying to achieve a dream he or she isn't passionate about. When people consider something precious, they treat it with care, and time is no exception. No one should squander it chasing a dream they aren't passionate about. Those who board the train to someone else's destination risk missing the ride to their own fulfillment. When you value time and pursue your goals with focus, you don't just reach a destination, you meet the purpose that was meant for you.

Decades before the iPhone was even imagined, those close to Steve Jobs recognized his extraordinary creativity. Chrisann Brennan, Jobs's early girlfriend and the mother of his first child, Lisa, recalled in her memoir that his inventive spirit was already evident in his twenties. She described how Jobs and Steve Wozniak built a device that allowed people to make free long-distance calls, a costly service at

---

169. Isaacson, Steve Jobs, 472

170. Steve Jobs, "My Favorite Things in Life Don't Cost Any Money. It's Really Clear That the Most Precious Resource We All Have Is Time," *BrainyQuote*, accessed June 20, 2025, https://www.brainyquote.com/quotes/steve_jobs_416854.

the time. The pair sold the devices to others, though Brennan noted she received hers free of charge.[171]

Steve Jobs thrived on creativity and execution, often leaving competitors scrambling to keep up. As Walter Isaacson observed, Jobs regularly brainstormed ideas with Apple executives to gather diverse perspectives.[172] But once he made a decision, changing his mind was nearly impossible. Biographers Brent Schlender and Rick Tetzeli noted that Jobs insisted a product must function well and look and feel right to him, regardless of whether competitors had already released similar offerings.[173] That unwavering standard became a cornerstone of Apple's success. Brennan's recollection revealed creativity and the early outlines of a leader who would demand excellence, resist compromise, and seek out only those who shared his vision.

Steve Jobs rejected fear and doubt, not only in himself but in those around him. As Walter Isaacson notes in the biography, he intentionally surrounded himself with like-minded individuals who believed deeply in his vision. Jobs sought passion, clarity, and conviction in his team, knowing that shared belief was essential to doing extraordinary work.[174]

This is one of the reasons he shook up Apple's board of directors in 1997.[175] It is also the reason behind the companies Apple partnered with—they had to believe in what Apple was doing. Steve Jobs knew if he wanted Apple to be successful, he needed positive and

---

171. Chrisann Brennan, *The Bite in the Apple: A Memoir of My Life with Steve Jobs* (New York: St. Martin's Press, 2013), 91–93.

172. Isaacson, *Steve Jobs*.

173. Schlender and Tetzeli, *Becoming Steve Jobs*, 327.

174. Isaacson, *Steve Jobs*.

175. "Jobs Names Apple Board," *CNN Money*, August 6, 1997, accessed June 20, 2025, https://money.cnn.com/1997/08/06/technology/apple/.

inspirational people to work with him. However, what if positive and inspirational people are not around to support and cheer you on? You let your goals inspire and motivate you to conquer your Goliath.

David hoped he would have positive people around him. He did not. However, that did not slow him or stop his run towards Goliath. And no one could stop him from executing his plan. He had no armor, no sword, and no backup. But he had belief, and belief doesn't flinch when giants roar.

STRATEGY 9 TAKEAWAYS

Saul and the Men in the Army	Steve Jobs and Teenager David
Avoided fighting for their future	Chose to fight for their future
Did not seek help to fight Goliath	Welcomed support beyond themselves
Lacked the passion to fight	Fought with boldness and belief

YOUR TURN TO REFLECT AND ACT

1. How will you rise and fight for your future with clarity and conviction?

2. Who can support you—and how will you invite them into your battle?

3. What will you do to fuel the passion that helps you fight and win?

Signature: _____ Today's date: _____

THE BEGINNING OF THE END

Visualize Your Success Before It Becomes Reality

Yea, though I walk through the valley of the shadow
of death, I will fear no evil: for thou art with me;
thy rod and thy staff they comfort me.

DAVID

David moves closer, eyes fixed on Goliath, feet pounding the hill like war drums. The giant can't believe the young guy's foolishness. It makes him angry. Maybe the boy has girl troubles and wants to numb the pain caused by heartbreak. It could even be the excess testosterone Goliath was told he had. But then Goliath notices the boy is slight and wiry, hardly a warrior's build. That can't be the reason, he thinks. Regardless, it doesn't matter why the boy wants to die. To Goliath, everything comes down to his goal, and that goal is death—the boy's death. There's no need to think about the boy's reasons.

The giant watches as the boy rapidly gets closer. He has to give it to him. He is braver than the Joker, Saul, and his so-called soldiers. Before long, he would grab the boy by the neck and separate his head from his body. The giant's long, fat fingers arch as they excitedly yearn to latch onto David's skinny neck.

Goliath wonders if the boy's brain can measure and register the pain. The boy probably would not feel much pain if he were killed too quickly. The giant thinks he might elevate the boy by his neck and gently but forcefully squeeze the breath from his body as he counts backward from nineteen to three. Maybe that's what it would take for Saul to show some respect and send him a real man to fight next time. The boy is much closer now; goodness, he is much smaller than the giant initially thought. Goliath spits in his hands and rubs them together as he awaits the clueless boy to arrive at the death chambers of his hands.

David can see that the giant is much bigger than he thought. *"What the heck did they feed this monster?"* he mutters to no one. David speculates that the big man's parents were just as huge. Oh, his poor mother. It must have been a traumatic labor for the woman as her body prepared itself to expel this monster. The poor woman's insides must have twisted and screamed in pain as she birthed this being. Goliath looks to be more of a beast than a human.

David wonders if Goliath has a wife or girlfriend. He imagines Goliath kissing the woman and her entire head disappearing into his mouth. What kind of woman would ever feel safe around such a creature, much less date him? David further imagines the woman in Goliath's life might just be tall enough to reach the giant's waist. He wonders how that would work when they did the "thing." Maybe Goliath sat while the woman stood on a stool so they could be eye-to-eye.

David envisions Goliath returning home, bloodied from battle after defeating his challengers. He wonders whether the giant's woman could stomach the carnage, and whether she cradled herself in his massive palm while washing the blood from his face. Then David imagines a different evening: the giant, sweaty but unbloodied, having found no one to fight. In his mind's eye, the woman runs to greet him, and Goliath lifts her into his arms effortlessly, with just two fingers.

He imagines Goliath sweating so profusely that sweat produces a warm shower for the woman. David then switches mental gears and wonders what the woman in Goliath's life would think when she heard he killed her man. How would she feel when she heard the news that he, a little teenager, had killed him? This thought intrigues David. He wonders if he would be attracted to Goliath's woman.

Would the woman want to meet him, David wonders? Would she be upset or relieved that he killed her man, the giant? Then again, David knows if the woman liked big men, she would not be attracted to him. However, he has a big heart. He wonders if that will count for anything. Women liked brave men, and like Goliath, he is brave. But all that didn't matter. If he does kill Goliath, and there is no doubt that he will, Saul will give him his daughter. A fierce thrill surges through David, electrifying his frame. He feels larger than life.

David imagines retiring from shepherding sheep to tending Saul's beautiful daughter, guiding her heart instead of a flock. He wonders what it feels like to trace her hair with his fingers, to know the warmth of her touch and the softness of her skin. He doesn't want to be their hero. He wants to be hers. He doesn't even know her name or what she looks like. In his mind, her eyes are lovely, her smile is inviting, and her embrace is welcoming. Desire stirs something primal in him. Then Goliath's monstrous face snaps him back to the moment.

He looks steadfastly at the giant.

DAVID UNFOLDS HIS PLAN

David knows this is the moment to transform his vision into reality. The giant looms before him, towering with intimidation, but retreating was never part of his plan. He had prepared and refined his strategy and now stood at the critical crossroads, where vision met action.

Great victories are never won by ideas alone; they demand execution. Plans without movement remain dreams, while those carried out with conviction transform into triumphs.

Great victories are never won by ideas alone; they demand execution. Plans without movement remain dreams, while those carried out with conviction transform into triumphs. In life, challenges will stare you down, daring you to falter, but success is reserved for those who act with purpose, precision, and unwavering belief. When the moment demands it, step forward, because a plan means nothing without action, and victory belongs to the bold.

The giant's large eyes fixate on the boy rushing toward him. He notices a quick movement, the stick slipping from the boy's hands. But he dismisses it with a scoff, thinking it's just clumsy nerves. His laughter grows louder, filled with disbelief and anger. All he focuses on is the boy's face. He doesn't see the hands or sense the change happening.

Goliath's armor bearer joins in the laughter and lowers the shield. What should have worried them both was that the boy didn't pick up the fallen stick. They didn't realize it was all part of David's clever plan. A thoughtful distraction to draw their attention away from his hands to prepare for the next move: the strike.

The final phase of David's plan is now ready to be executed. Still running, David reaches into his shepherd's bag and retrieves the kill-stone. This stone would do what the spears of many men had failed to do, kill Goliath. The stone would be unseen by Goliath's armor bearer, so he could not divert it with his shield. Goliath himself would not see it until it was tragically too late. Without displaying emotion or intent and without Goliath's huge eyes noticing, David slips the stone into his sling.

Saul and the soldiers hold their collective breath. They watch from behind as David runs towards Goliath. They cannot see the boy's expressionless face. However, they see Goliath's face, and what they see sinks them deeper into the abyss of hopelessness.

Goliath's face is adorned with a familiar yet unsettling mixture of amusement, anger, intrigue, and unwavering confidence. He looks like a ravenous lion, poised to strike, his predatory gaze locked onto his prey, ready to devour without hesitation. He looks like he is contemplating whether he would eat David alive or shred him to pieces with his teeth.

Dread, dismay, and despair bleed from David's brothers' hearts as extreme fear grips and squeezes their emotions. *What had Saul done? What had they done? What had they allowed?* Their father would never forgive them. They knew he didn't think much of David, but still, he was his last son. How had they allowed their youngest brother to face and attempt to fight the most fearsome enemy Israel ever encountered?

Buckets of tears unashamedly empty down their faces as they know what is about to happen, or so they think. They had seen what Goliath did to his victims, and it was not a sight for the fainthearted. They couldn't see their youngest brother's face, but if they had, their shock would have deepened.

David's facial expression does not reveal his burning animosity towards the giant. To Goliath, he is a nobody who disrespected him by even thinking he could fight and kill him. Goliath thinks that if David had been a legitimate threat, he would have previously heard about him. But this was the first time he saw and became aware of the boy. Goliath couldn't believe he wasted forty days and forty nights waiting for this. Was this the best Saul could do? Again, the giant bellows in laughter as excessive saliva gallops from his mouth, insulting the grass. Yet, for some inexplicable reason, the boy is still running towards him. This doesn't make sense to the giant, but he welcomes it—wrongly.

DAVID EXECUTES HIS PLAN

Goliath's thoughts are interrupted by what seems to be the boy tripping and trying to regain his balance. The boy is flailing his arms as if attempting to correct his misstep. Laughter finds the giant's mouth once again, and he can hardly contain himself. What a joke, he thinks. But what the giant does not know is that David did not trip. The giant's perspective was incorrect. It was way off. He does not know David is setting up his final move by transferring the stone from his shepherd's bag to its temporary residence on the sling. Now the stone is in the sling and being prepared for takeoff to the giant's head, and then to its final home—Goliath's forehead. The sling moves in a circular motion as David initiates an action that would produce inaction in the giant.

Even though his eyes are bigger than those of anyone around, the giant cannot see what David is doing. All he sees is an unbalanced boy about to fall. Goliath moves his massive body down the mountain slope towards David. He envisions that he would bring his right foot down hard on his neck once the boy falls like a judge slamming a gavel to seal one's fate.

The giant wonders if this action will detach the boy's head from his body. But then again, he does not want the youngster to die so quickly. He wants him to suffer for insulting his reputation. He likes it when people praise him for killing big men. What glory would he get for killing this little boy who now seemed to be spaced out? Yes, he would make the boy die slowly. He would break every bone in his body and try to make a fire with them.

DAVID USES THE STONE TO TOPPLE THE GIANT

Goliath misinterpreted David's intense focus on the task at hand. The youngster's ears seemed to have turned off because he no longer heard external sounds. He was no longer looking at the giant, per se. David's eyes zeroed in on one location, the center of the giant's forehead. And without further hesitation, David did what he had been planning all along. He blasted the stone from his sling towards Goliath's forehead with optimal precision and impeccable timing. The stone cut through the air with such blinding speed, seemingly similar to the NASA/USAF X-15, the fastest hypersonic experimental aircraft, reaching speeds of up to 4,520 mph, more than five times faster than the speed of sound (Mach 6).[176]

Fortunately for Goliath, his brain did not possess the GHz processor speed capable of analyzing the stone's stunning and painful impact. If it did, he would have experienced pain like he had inflicted on so many. Upon its arrival, the stone quickly and painfully constructed

176. Liam McInerney, "World's Fastest Plane Could Have Reached New York from London in 45 Minutes," *Express*, February 8, 2025, accessed June 20, 2025, https://www.express.co.uk/news/world/2011012/worlds-fastest-plane-4520mph.

an opening at the exact location David had been scouting moments earlier. The smooth, oval-shaped stone violently cut, pierced, and entered the middle of the giant's forehead. One might have argued that the stone could have been prosecuted for piercing and entering with the sole intent to kill.

It happened so quickly to Goliath, yet he saw it in slow motion. Goliath saw the stone's forceful arrival before it entered his forehead, but his brain did not have enough time to signal the huge head to move out of the way. His giant brain was confused about an immediate course of action, so it gave up. Goliath's armor bearer heard a swoosh and then a crushing sound as the stone made its piercing acquaintance with the giant's forehead.

The armor bearer looks back at the giant and notices something is dreadfully amiss. Goliath has this stunned and unbelievable expression, and there is a hole in the middle of his forehead. *What the hell just happened?* The armor bearer had never seen Goliath in such a fashion. The shield falls from the armor bearer's hands as his body shakes and weakens. The blood on his face rushes elsewhere in his body and hides. Never was this sight seen, not by him nor anyone else. As he gazes in bewilderment at Goliath's current state, the armor bearer's brain unsuccessfully tries to process what his eyes see.

The day had begun like any other day. Goliath had used the same routine for the past forty days. He had been with Goliath for the past forty days. He had defended the giant against many spears that sought to end the giant's life prior to the forty days. He had witnessed the giant's great exploits for several years. Now, obviously, the giant was exploited. There was no other way to spin it. The youngster had done to the giant what no other man was able to do—for years. "*This can't be happening,*" the armor bearer thought.

Meanwhile, the Philistine soldiers stand frozen in shock as Goliath falls uncharacteristically silent. His mouth is wide open, yet no words escape. The giant seems suspended, not by ropes, but by a mind that cannot decide. He hung between the here-life and the afterlife. Never had they seen their champion act in such an unorthodox manner. Initially, the Philistine soldiers did not grasp what had happened to their champion. They did not realize Goliath was involuntarily positioning himself to make his final and permanent bow. His best-selling, long-running one-man show was undoubtedly and unexpectedly canceled. It was shut down by the most unlikely foe, utilizing the most unlikely means. The undisputed underdog, the boy with the stick whom he had laughed at and cursed, had permanently silenced him.

From their vantage point, Saul and his men eventually saw what David was trying to do. Israelites occasionally practiced and fought using a sling and a stone as a weapon.[177] However, they find it increasingly hard to believe the boy pulled it off. But what happens next makes them question what they're seeing, not just the onlookers, but David's brothers and even the eyes of the Philistines.

Suddenly, the nine-foot monster named Goliath did not look so intimidating anymore. The stone had disrupted his fearsomeness. The violence and threats that once resided in his eyes and gushed from his mouth had gone out of business. The freak of nature who had terrorized the Israelites for forty days and forty nights and for so many others for many years had lost his luster. Once the tormentor, now the tormented, he looked undone by the very fear he used to command. It would only get worse—devastatingly worse.

---

177. David's Sling and Stones—Were They Toys or Serious Weapons?" *ChristianAnswers.net*, accessed June 20, 2025, https://christiananswers.net/q-abr/abr-slingsforkids.html.

What happens next results in a nightmare for the Philistines and unbelievably victorious screams from Saul and his men. To David, it is what he had envisioned. He knew he would accomplish this goal when Saul gave him the chance.

As the stone crashed through Goliath's frontal lobe, his judgment was interrupted, and his memory of standing was lost. He began displaying characteristics like a giant sequoia tree quickly cut at its base. Goliath, the warlord, the man who had caused such fear and terror in Saul and his men, started to fall forward. It was unbelievable. It was a sight to behold.

Like hovering drones, birds froze midair, their wings suspended as they took in the scene below. On the ground, hidden creatures peeked cautiously from their burrows, unwilling to miss the moment that decided everything—Goliath lay defeated. They knew they were witnessing a once-in-a-lifetime event. And within a few seconds after the initial downward movement, Goliath's body hit and shook the earth with such force that the dirt gave way to welcome its new guest.

Suddenly, fear transferred all its files from Saul and his men to Goliath's armor bearer and soldiers. And in a synchronous fashion, confidence, utilizing fiber optic speeds, darted from the Philistines to Saul and his men. By now, David, still running, arrived at Goliath's body shortly after it violently kissed the ground.

Victory is never a single moment, it's a process.

David was not finished. He had one more task: he needed to add the crescendo to his performance. He had to do what he had promised the giant. David lunged at Goliath's body faster than the speed he used to catch and kill the lion that had ripped one of his sheep away from the flock.

Victory is never a single moment, it's a process. David had struck Goliath down, but his mission was not yet complete. Triumph is not merely in the act of execution, but in the follow-through that ensures success is solidified. Like a warrior finishing the final strike, a leader sealing a deal, or an artist perfecting the last brushstroke, true victory requires commitment beyond the initial achievement. Many falter after landing the first blow, assuming the battle is won. Success isn't just claimed, it's conquered. It demands relentless persistence, razor-sharp precision, and the unwavering drive to finish what you started.

The giant was not dead, just stunned and unconscious. David knew he needed to execute one final act before the curtain of victory was closed. This act would ripple shock among all those who witnessed it. Those who witnessed it would never forget what they saw. No one would ever look at David the same again, not even his brothers, who thought they knew their youngest brother well.

What they saw would be retold for generations by men, birds, and animals. Men would brag to others that they were there and saw it. They would recount the moment Goliath fell. However, what David did next seized their attention. It was raw, predictable, yet unpredictable. It was something to behold. One had to see it as words became inadequate to effectively capture and record what next occurred.

David immediately saw what he was looking for. He grabbed it and began. The Philistines could not believe their eyes were telling the truth. Saul and his men no longer blinked because of what the boy was now doing. They saw the giant had fallen face down, but what they witnessed next shocked them.

It shocked them to their military core. After this action, there was no way the giant Goliath would ever recover. What David was now doing to his competitor left no doubt. Like David, when Steve Jobs executed his plans at Apple, there was no doubt that many of his competitors would not recover.

STEVE JOBS DELIVERED
SHOCK TO HIS COMPETITORS

Steve Jobs knew that to build Apple into a formidable company, he needed to constantly shock his competitors. Shocking them would keep them off balance by disrupting their revenue and keeping them behind Apple's technological advances.

Like David with a stone, Jobs returned to Apple with only a vision and a name, but wielded them with deadly precision. At first, he was just an advisor, a presence behind the scenes. But to slay the corporate Goliaths and resurrect Apple's identity, he needed more than influence, he needed control.

Isaacson writes that Jobs "became Apple's interim CEO in 1997" and swiftly restructured the board, aligning its leadership with his mission.[178] From that moment, Apple's slingshot was drawn. The iPhone would be the smooth stone that took flight.

By 2007, when Jobs unveiled the iPhone, he stunned the tech world. Research In Motion stood dazed, like Goliath blinking in disbelief, still believing himself mighty. But the stone had struck true, and though the collapse would come later, its fall had already begun.[179] Just like that, the giant stumbled, and the shepherd seized the moment.

The giant music industry was stunned when Steve Jobs introduced

---

178. Isaacson, *Steve Jobs*, 317-321.

179. Research In Motion Limited. 2012. "Annual Information Form." *U.S. Securities and Exchange Commission*, April 9, 2012. Accessed April 7, 2025. https://www.sec.gov/Archives/edgar/data/1070235/000119312512155342/d253804dex11.htm.

the iPod and released iTunes. But Jobs didn't just disrupt the status quo, he destroyed it. Record labels no longer saw value in bundling albums; consumers no longer needed to buy physical records. With an iPod in their pocket and iTunes on their screen, music lovers could collect songs one at a time, on their own terms.[180]

Steve Jobs didn't just reimagine technology, he restructured entire industries. The iPhone disrupted newsrooms, gutted the desktop market, and shook the foundations of traditional television through Apple TV.[181] Jobs and Apple dismantled the norms that their competitors once controlled. With every iDevice release, another Goliath fell.

Those rivals, like the Philistine giant, once stood tall and untouchable. But now, their dominance lay shattered, overthrown not by brute force, but by vision made real. And just as David stood over his foe, Jobs ensured the defeated stayed down.

Both men had a plan. They executed it. And they won.

---

180. Isaacson, *Steve Jobs*, 394-410.

181. Tim Bajarin, "How Apple's iPhone Changed These 5 Major Industries," *Time*, June 26, 2017, accessed June 20, 2025, https://time.com/4832599/iphone-anniversary-industry-change/.

STRATEGY 10 TAKEAWAYS

Saul and the Men in the Army	Steve Jobs and Teenager David
Failed to create a plan	Developed a clear strategy
Took no option	Executed their plan with purpose
Ended in failure	Achieved meaningful success

YOUR TURN TO REFLECT AND ACT

1. What plans will you craft to face and defeat the Goliaths in your life?

2. How will you put those plans into motion with confidence and discipline?

3. What habits, mindset, or support will help you stay on the path to success?

Signature: _____ Today's date: _____

THE END IS OVER

Finish What You Started

*Be a yardstick of quality. Some people aren't used to
an environment where excellence is expected.*
STEVE JOBS

David quickly pulls Goliath's sword from its sheath. The young-ster is in his own world and does not notice Saul and the Israel-ite soldiers as they cautiously edge closer. As they move closer, Saul and his men see dust particles take flight as the giant's enormous nostrils release carbon dioxide, disturbing their rest. After such a fall, they find it hard to believe the giant is not dead. Up close, and even though he is in a horizontal position, face down, they are still scared. He is the largest human being their eyes have ever beheld. They won-der if his birth certificate documents an earthly birth. What David does next is realign their thoughts.

David violently grabs the giant's long hair and yanks his head awk-wardly, exposing his thick neck. Fueled with the adrenaline of excite-ment and passion, David sets to work. In rapid motion, he introduces Goliath's own sword to the side of the big man's neck.

The sharp edge of the sword painfully and passionately kisses the giant's neck like a long-missed lover. And like a violin player, David uses the sword like a bow. He moves it back and forth upon the giant's neck as blood applauds his hands. The sword's crushing melody serenades Goliath's skin, nerves, muscles, ligaments, and tendons with multiple crescendos. And as suddenly as it started, the performance abruptly ends as *David drops the sword.* The sword hits the dirt. Goliath's head and body no longer share the union they enjoyed for decades. To illustrate this discord, David uses two hands and raises the giant's head so that all can see as the blood of victory serenades his body. He has skillfully navigated his first surgery, without any medical training. He separated the giant's head from its body.

David, the boy Saul initially thought could never defeat Goliath, now lifts the giant's head high. Goliath's eyes are wide open, as if he wants to witness the fresh blood running from his neck. He unconsciously stares directly ahead. However, it is obvious no one is home. Goliath is long gone before he knows his spirit left on an early, unscheduled flight. His face freezes into a perfect portrait of shock and disbelief, his forehead pressed tightly against the smooth, oval stone.

Saul and his soldiers roar in stunned triumph. They rush and lift David as they sing and shout in three-part harmony, "*You killed the giant.*" "*You killed the giant.*" "*You killed the giant.*" At that moment, the Philistine soldiers grasp the shocking reality of their champion's fall—and respond just as expected. As they witness the boy humiliate and behead Goliath, panic ripples through their ranks. Gripped by sheer terror, they flee for their lives, running for the first time, unacquainted with the sting of defeat.

For forty days, they had watched the Israelites fearfully run from Goliath. Now, it is their turn to run, and they do. They run, hoping their feet will turn back the hands of time and bring their champion,

Goliath, back to life. In one sense, their run turned back the hands of time for Saul and his soldiers.

YOUR VICTORY WILL INSPIRE OTHERS

David's victory wasn't just his, it became a force that reignited the strength within those who had forgotten their own power. The sight of the fallen giant was more than proof of success; it was a declaration that fear was no longer in command. Courage, once buried beneath doubt, erupted with newfound force. The soldiers, who had once trembled at Goliath's mere presence, now felt something surge within them, a reminder of who they truly were.

Like flames ignited by a single spark, their resolve spread through the ranks. Fear had been exiled, and a warrior's instinct replaced hesitation. The battlefield was no longer a place of retreat, it became a proving ground for the strength they had thought lost. Once silenced by uncertainty, their voices roared through the valley, shaking the earth like the thunderous engines of war-bound fighter jets.

David's triumph had transformed the impossible into the inevitable. His courage had not only won the battle but also awakened something deep within Saul and the soldiers.

A single victory can turn doubt into courage.
When you rise, others remember how to stand.

A single victory can turn doubt into courage. When you rise, others remember how to stand. They had been spectators in their own war, but now, their warrior's spirit was revived. Their lost courage returns, and their weakness is evicted by strength. Fear that had once crippled them releases its grip. It had taken sudden leave as when darkness is hit by light. This stunning turnaround is clear as their battle cries fill and shake the air like F16 fighter jets taking off. And they take off against the Philistine soldiers.

The Israelite soldiers pursue the Philistines like angry and hungry lions pursuing their prey. They chase them through the Israelite city of Shaaraim back to the Philistine city of Gath. They kill the Philistines along the plains and valleys and leave their bodies scattered like fertilizer.

The vision of David's courageous and bloody act reinforces the soldiers' resolve. Like David, they have no mercy on the Philistines who had stood behind the fearsome Goliath. After all, they are soldiers and warriors, and they would remind the Philistines of that fact. Thanks to the brave boy, they were back at the top of their game.

YOUR VICTORY WILL ENERGIZE OTHERS

When you fight and defeat Goliaths, it's not just for your benefit. You inspire others. To some, you are like a pilot. Your actions during the turbulence of life will either calm their fears or heighten their stress.

A pilot's calm announcement is one of the most comforting things to me during a flight. For some reason, I seem to listen for panic in a pilot's voice when unexpected turbulence is announced. To me, this is often more significant than what the pilot is saying.

The passengers will panic if a pilot sounds frightened and nervous when announcing turbulence. Pilots are trained to remain calm and sound calm during turbulence.[182] By remaining calm, they are likely to think clearly, act responsibly during emergencies, and not cause

---

182. David Dale, "How Does a Pilot Remain Calm Under Pressure?" *Avgeekery*, July 7, 2024, accessed June 20, 2025, https://avgeekery.com/pilots-calm-in-cockpit/.

passengers to panic. Once they adhere to their training, it is less likely that their passengers will panic after hearing an announcement in a calm and authoritative voice.

This applies to just about all walks of life. How parents respond to different situations is a lesson children will learn well. Children learn a lot in the classroom about thinking and solving educational challenges. However, they learn about life at home from parents, grandparents, siblings, and guardians. They learn to be calm and how to navigate life. Imagine a child who is afraid of the dark having a parent who is also afraid of the dark and verbalizing it. It takes a parent to show empathy, patience, and understanding for the child to rectify the situation. How one responds to other leadership roles is significant and can often determine success or failure.

Saul's leadership actions significantly and negatively affected his soldiers when he saw Goliath. Saul was extremely afraid when he saw Goliath and heard his threats. This was a natural emotion because Goliath was fearsome. However, one key mistake Saul made as a leader was to show his fear. Because he did this, all his soldiers, looking to him for guidance, saw fear. Furthermore, they also became extremely fearful because they saw fear in the leader.

If Saul had masked his fear and faked confidence, his soldiers might have felt they had a chance against the fearsome challenger. One soldier might have even mustered the courage to volunteer to fight Goliath.

Always displaying confidence is extremely important, whether you are a parent, teacher, coach, or business leader. This constant display of confidence can and should become a habit. While life is not without issues and challenges, you can train your mind and emotions always to reflect confidence through your body. One way to train the mind in this aspect is to constantly reassure yourself that situations will work out. Your first response should be optimism, not pessimism.

OPTIMISM IS A KEY INGREDIENT OF SUCCESS

An optimistic attitude will yield optimistic results. A constant optimistic attitude will affect your body language and position you for success. This is true for just about any situation. Regardless of the challenges and issues you face personally or professionally, always remain optimistic. See yourself winning even when it looks like you are losing. One's attitude has a significant bearing on the outcome. Consistently maintaining and displaying a positive attitude despite challenges is a great idea. Scientific studies support this notion. They reveal it is beneficial to fake it till you make it.

FAKE IT 'TILL YOU MAKE IT

Social psychologist Amy Cuddy noted the relationships between body poses and how they affect perception and action. In a TED speech, she explained that people's body language determines how others view them and how they view themselves.[183] She cemented this by suggesting people should project themselves based on their intended outcome. According to Cuddy, exhibiting a confident posture (upright shoulders, protruded chest, head held high, etc.) will positively affect one's behavior. It will, in turn, lead to positive outcomes.

Would you hire someone for a customer service position who came to the interview with drooped shoulders and negative vibes? Would you go on a date with someone who approaches you and never

183. Amy Cuddy, *Your Body Language May Shape Who You Are*, TED Talk, TEDGlobal 2012, filmed June 2012, posted October 2012, accessed June 20, 2025, https://www.ted.com/talks/amy_cuddy_your_body_language_may_shape_who_you_are.

makes eye contact? You likely answered "no" to both questions. Why? First, because of the interviewee's body language, you know he or she would not likely be an asset to your business. Regarding the person who asked for the date, you might be turned off by a lack of confidence or ponder what the person was hiding. These support Cuddy's claim that displaying an uncertain and pessimistic posture (head held down, slouched stance, etc.) will likely lead to unwanted outcomes. Make a concerted effort always to exude confidence, even if you do not feel confident.

Leadership communication doesn't just begin with words—it starts with posture, poise, and presence. CNBC writer Marguerite Ward outlined seven body language habits that confident leaders use to command attention: making eye contact, talking with their hands, sitting and standing upright, resisting the urge to fidget, avoiding crossed legs (especially for women), and maintaining a calm, even tone of voice. Through examples of successful public figures, Ward illustrates that confidence is often performed before it's felt. The implication? Projecting strength can pave the way for believing in it.[184]

This is as true for business leaders as it is for parents. This strategy would have been beneficial for Saul and his men.

DAVID'S CONFIDENCE SET UP HIS SUCCESS

When Saul and the Israelite soldiers ran away from Goliath and cowered in fear, they set themselves up to fail. However, David's confident talk and positive body language jump-started the journey to the winning side. David was only ushered into Saul's office because

---

184. Marguerite Ward, "7 Body-Language Tricks to Exude Confidence," *CNBC*, September 14, 2016, accessed June 20, 2025, https://www.cnbc.com/2016/09/14/7-body-language-tricks-to-exude-confidence.html.

of his confidence. The soldiers saw the confidence in David that they lacked. They were dressed for war, yet they brought a boy to Saul to represent them in battle against the giant.

> Confidence doesn't just open doors,
> it commands them to swing wide.

David's confidence created the opportunity to meet with the highest military leader in Israel at the time. It is worth mentioning again that Saul's soldiers escorted David into Saul's very presence. David did not ask to speak with Saul. Saul's soldiers, who should have accepted Goliath's challenge, escorted the armor-less non-soldier to the interview. To the soldiers, the boy was their only hope—his unwavering confidence set him apart.

Confidence doesn't just open doors, it commands them to swing wide. David's belief in his ability turned him from an unnoticed shepherd into a warrior of influence. He didn't beg for recognition; his certainty in victory made others see what they had overlooked. Confidence is the force that shifts perception, creates opportunity, and positions you for success. It isn't arrogance—it's assurance, the unwavering resolve that silence has no place when the battle calls. Confidence isn't just belief, it's the key that unlocks success. Step forward, and watch the world make way.

IS YOUR SUCCESS AWAITING YOUR CONFIDENCE?

Psychologist Dr. Barbara Markway lists five benefits of self-confidence:

- **Less Fear and Anxiety:** Confidence helps calm your inner critic and reduces overthinking, leading to less fear and anxiety.

- **Greater Motivation:** Self-confidence increases your drive to set and achieve meaningful goals.

- **More Resilience:** With confidence, you can manage setbacks and failures more effectively.

- **Improved Relationships:** When you're self-assured, you engage more genuinely with others, leading to better relationships.

- **Stronger Sense of Your Authentic Self:** Confidence allows you to embrace your strengths and weaknesses, giving you a stronger sense of your true self.[185]

You want the best for your children, so you invest your time and money to make that happen. You compliment them and encourage them to build their confidence. This is admirable. However, let me ask: do you want the best for yourself? Do you invest time, money, and confidence-building skills in yourself?

Act today to increase your confidence. Author and Entrepreneur. com contributor Jacqueline Whitmore lists six daily actions to build self-confidence:

- **Act confident:** Your body language sends powerful signals. Stand tall, make eye contact, and carry yourself as if you already belong in the room. When you *look* confident, others respond accordingly, and your mindset often follows.

---

185. Barbara Markway, "Why Self-Confidence Is More Important Than You Think," *Psychology Today*, September 20, 2018, accessed June 20, 2025, https://www.psychologytoday.com/us/blog/shyness-is-nice/201809/why-self-confidence-is-more-important-you-think.

- **Dress successfully and let your attire reflect your confidence:** Clothing influences how you feel and how others perceive you. Wearing well-fitted, appropriate attire that reflects your personality can elevate your self-esteem and signal readiness.

- **Speak confidently:** Use a steady, clear tone. Avoid filler words like "um" or "you know," and embrace pauses to emphasize key points. Speaking with intention shows you believe in what you're saying, and invites others to believe it too.

- **Think and act positively:** Confidence thrives in a positive mindset. Replace self-doubt with affirmations, surround yourself with uplifting people, and focus on what's possible rather than what's lacking.

- **Practice being self-confident:** Confidence is a skill, not a trait. Step into unfamiliar situations, take small risks, and stretch your comfort zone. Each success builds your internal proof that you can handle more.

- **Be prepared in the area you want to succeed:** Preparation breeds confidence. Whether it's a presentation, interview, or conversation, knowing your material and anticipating challenges gives you the calm assurance to perform at your best.[186]

Making these habits a daily occurrence will quicken your steps to success. Let's look at David and see how he measured up to these steps.

---

186. Whitmore, Jacqueline. "6 Actions You Can Take Every Day to Build Your Self-Confidence." *Entrepreneur*, June 16, 2015. Accessed April 7, 2025. https://www.entrepreneur.com/living/6-actions-you-can-take-every-day-to-build-your/299836.

While David did not lack self-confidence, he displayed all six steps Whitmore listed. You might argue he was not dressed for success since he did not wear Saul's armor. That is a valid point. However, looking closely, you will see David was indeed attired to succeed. Remember, he had his shepherd's bag containing the stone, and he had his sling. Furthermore, David knew he would be using Goliath's sword. I would argue that David was well-dressed for success. What are your thoughts?

On the other hand, Saul and his men only took one of Whitmore's six steps. They were dressed for success; that is it. Saul and his soldiers only took 17 percent of the steps needed to build their self-confidence (according to Whitmore's template), so it is no wonder they ran away in fear.

What percentage of Whitmore steps do you use? You may already be confident and successful; however, making the six steps a daily habit will boost your self-confidence and success. Please do it for you. Many more successes are awaiting your increased self-confidence. Make these steps habitual, keep a positive attitude, always display confident body language, and grab your successes. The only caveat is that you manage your confidence level to the extent that it does not hurt you. In other words, too much confidence can be a disadvantage.

OVERCONFIDENCE CAN BE DANGEROUS

Overconfidence can be detrimental to one's success. Before I produce evidence to support this statement, let's spend a few sentences investigating Goliath's over-the-top confidence level. I will show how the giant's overconfidence led to his defeat. We learned from Saul that Goliath was a warrior since he was David's age. Moreover, the fact that Goliath was referred to as a champion of the Philistines meant he was their most successful fighter. He was the undisputed champion and top fighter. Goliath won all his fights and was considered unbeatable.

In today's terminology, Goliath would have been the reigning heavyweight boxing champion of the world. Recall that Israel's trained soldiers were scared to fight Goliath. Let's consider that Goliath was more than three feet taller than former heavyweight world champions Muhammad Ali, Mike Tyson, and Lennox Lewis. The giant likely weighed over 800 pounds. He was a heinous monster.

His size was so intimidating that just the sight of him caused extreme fear in Saul and the soldiers. Moreover, Goliath's reputation preceded him. No one in that part of the world was unaware of Goliath's exploits. Goliath did not just kill men. He massacred them. He violently ripped and rearranged his victims' internal and external organs. The giant did not know the word "mercy." He was from a family of fearsome warriors. Because of all these characteristics, Goliath's confidence level was immeasurable.

No wonder he was offended when he saw his younger, smaller challenger. David did not fit his profile of a worthwhile opponent at all. As such, Goliath did not view David as a serious opponent or threat. The giant's confidence soared even more when he realized David would attempt to fight him.

Goliath's confidence heightened and ballooned, and his defenses rapidly abated. David expected this and used it to his advantage. Had Goliath not been so blatantly overconfident, perhaps his mind would have warned him: *Never underestimate the underdog.* Confidence must be governed wisely, otherwise, it turns from strength to stumbling block.

THE PERILS OF OVERCONFIDENCE

Psychologist Dr. Bobby Hoffman warns that overconfidence can lead to serious, and sometimes tragic—consequences. He cites historical examples such as the 1876 Battle of the Little Bighorn, where Colonel George Armstrong Custer, brimming with self-assurance, ordered an attack on the Cheyenne warriors. The result was a devastating massacre of federal troops. Hoffman also references the sinking of the Titanic, attributing part of the disaster to the ship captain's overconfidence in the vessel's supposed invincibility, which led to a delayed response after the iceberg strike.[187]

SCIENTIFIC EVIDENCE OF THE
DANGERS OF OVERCONFIDENCE

Hoffman defines overconfidence in scientific terms as *myside bias*—the tendency to overestimate one's abilities or judgments based on personal belief rather than objective evidence. He offers relatable examples: missing project deadlines due to unrealistic expectations, or overestimating one's driving skills, which can lead to risky behavior on the road.[188]

Building on Hoffman's insights, it's worth noting that this kind of overconfidence is especially common among teenage boys. During adolescence, rising testosterone levels and a developing sense of identity can amplify self-assurance, particularly behind the wheel. This may help explain why insurance rates for teen males are often higher: confidence, when unchecked by experience, can become a liability.

There were times I could have lost my life as a teenage driver.

---

187. Bobby Hoffman, "When You Have Too Much Confidence, Expect This to Happen," *Psychology Today*, August 17, 2017, accessed June 20, 2025, https://www.psychologytoday.com/us/blog/motivate/201708/when-you-have-too-much-confidence-expect-this-to-happen.

188. *Ibid.*

However, let me tell you about an incident where my overconfidence left me with a seriously bruised ego. I attended high school on the Caribbean Island of Jamaica and was overconfident about my riding abilities. My friend had a new bicycle, and my overconfidence screamed at me that I was an expert rider.

After school one day, I asked my friend if I could ride his bike. I mounted the ride and was doing well—until I saw three girls. Suddenly, my overconfidence jolted my feet and strengthened my hands. I sped up by the girls, and as I passed them, I decided I could skillfully and seductively weave the bike from side to side. In other words, I wanted to show off.

For some inexplicable reason, I forgot about the laws of gravity and that I was not that good of a rider. I ended up on the ground with several bruises. I must confess that the bruises did not hurt as much as the girls' laughter. To say I was embarrassed is an understatement. My ego was severely damaged.

Dr. Hoffman comprehensively defines myside bias. In order to fully capture his comprehensive definition, I will directly quote:

Myside bias usually means not being able to see the potential drawbacks of your own personal beliefs and perspectives. In the worst case, bias results in poor decisions because we only seek out evidence that confirms our pre-existing beliefs, clouding our analytical skills and interfering with our ability to solve problems correctly.[189]

One might argue that Steve Jobs sometimes suffered from myside bias. His unwavering confidence sometimes clouded judgment and hurt Apple's bottom line. Still, as mentioned earlier, when he returned in 1997 and trimmed a bloated, unfocused product line, he showed

189. *Ibid.*, 149.

he could prune even the limbs he once helped grow. Jobs surrounded himself with sharp minds who challenged his thinking, and he listened. As *Inc.* magazine notes, this ability to overcome cognitive traps like the endowment effect (a close cousin to myside bias) was key to Apple's remarkable transformation.[190]

STEVE JOBS AND MYSIDE BIAS

Psychologist Dr. Bobby Hoffman warns that unchecked overconfidence can have significant consequences, a pattern also seen in some of the world's most celebrated innovators. One such case is Steve Jobs, whose remarkable successes often fueled a level of confidence that bordered on distortion. His colleagues famously referred to his strong belief in his own vision as a "reality distortion field." [191]

Walter Isaacson recounts how this overconfidence occasionally led to clashes with engineers and vendors at Apple, disrupting workflows and delaying progress. A striking example is the 1984 Macintosh: Jobs insisted the machine didn't need a large internal hard drive or substantial memory. Convinced his minimalist vision would prevail, he ignored technical feedback. But customers disagreed. The Mac's initial sales faltered, revealing how even brilliant foresight can stumble when it's not balanced by realism.[192]

CONFIDENCE WITHOUT COMPROMISE

Biographers Brent Schlender and Rick Tetzeli observed that Steve Jobs often held unwavering faith in his own ideas, so much so that

190. Jeff Haden, "28 Years Ago, Steve Jobs Overcame This Cognitive Bias to Completely Transform Apple," *Inc.*, May 27, 2025, https://www.inc.com/jeff-haden/28-years-ago-steve-jobs-overcame-this-cognitive-bias-to-completely-transform-apple/91193354

191. Isaacson, *Steve Jobs*, 117-118.

192. Isaacson, *Steve Jobs*, 186.

he was frequently unwilling to compromise. This deep-seated confidence sometimes led to tensions with senior Apple colleagues and proved counterproductive to collaboration and progress.[193]

Yet, Schlender and Tetzeli also point out that Jobs evolved. When he moved beyond what might be called a *myside bias*—tuning out alternative perspectives—and instead leaned into his "inner voice," he made some of his most impactful decisions. It's in these moments of balance between conviction and openness that his leadership truly flourished.

This held true for David as well. Neither he nor Steve Jobs could have accomplished what they did without first tuning in to their authentic inner voice—the quiet conviction that guided their boldest decisions. You and I possess that same voice. It's universal, embedded in all living beings, and when we choose to listen, it leads us to purpose, growth, and often the extraordinary.

A baby isn't taught how to breathe, cry, crawl, or walk. These instincts arise from an innate voice, what some might call nature, others the soul. And while we may falter or act in self-interest at times, I believe that inner voice also calls us to rise, serve, and create lasting value for others.

So the question becomes: Will we listen? Like David and Jobs, our most significant strides may begin the moment we do.

---

193. Brent Schlender and Rick Tetzeli, *Becoming Steve Jobs: The Evolution of a Reckless Upstart into a Visionary Leader* (New York: Crown Business, 2015), 278.

STRATEGY 11 TAKEAWAYS

Saul and the Men in the Army	Steve Jobs and Teenager David
Retreated in fear	Advanced with confidence
Avoided facing the issue	Confronted the challenge directly
Failed to resolve the problem	Finished what they started

YOUR TURN TO REFLECT AND ACT

1. What is your plan to move forward with purpose and confidence?

2. How will you confront and navigate life's toughest challenges?

3. What commitments will you make to ensure you finish strong—no matter what?

Signature: _____ Today's date: _____

THE TRUTH VALUE

Rewrite Your Future, Defy Your Past

> *Let's go invent tomorrow instead of worrying*
> *about what happened yesterday.*
> **STEVE JOBS**

reating value for others will inevitably create value for yourself. You've already seen how Steve Jobs, who was adopted, misunderstood, and dismissed, used his past not as a reason to retreat but as fuel to build one of the most influential companies in the world. And how David, armed only with faith and resolve, rose from shepherd to sovereign by choosing service over self. These men didn't wait for ideal conditions. They created value in the middle of uncertainty, and in doing so, redefined what was possible. So can you. Your past doesn't disqualify you; it prepares you.

The question is no longer *what have you been through?* but *what will you build because of it?*

DAVID CREATED VALUE FOR MANY, INCLUDING HIMSELF

You will recall that David's major beef with Goliath was his statement that the giant was devaluing the Israelites and their God. The first thing David says upon hearing Goliath is a question—he wants to know what reward will be given to the one who defeats the giant and ends the disgrace. While David inquired about the reward for defeating Goliath, it became clear that the driving force behind his decision wasn't the prize, it was silencing the giant and restoring dignity to the Israelites. This is evident throughout the story: David never mentions the reward again. Instead, he repeatedly voices his outrage at Goliath's taunts.

It's reasonable to assert that David would have fought the giant even without an incentive. His motivation was greater than personal gain, it was about protecting his people and honoring his family. His victory would (1) deliver Israel from the grip of Goliath's tyranny, and (2) exempt his family from taxes in Israel. And yes, he also received Saul's daughter as a wife, but David's greatness wasn't in what he gained. It was in what he gave: courage, clarity, and conviction in the face of fear. His legacy flows from the values he lived, not the rewards he collected.

UNLEASH YOUR GREATNESS AND CREATE VALUE

There is no doubt that there is greatness in you. God has embedded greatness in your DNA. However, people often misjudge you by their biases and because of your mess-ups. Nevertheless, only you truly know the desires and drive that accelerate the passions flowing through your heart. Do not let the negative perception of others define you. Do not let the mistakes of your past or your present define you. No one is without mistakes, failures, even the most successful person.

David's journey to victory didn't begin on the battlefield, it started with dismissing his doubters and the doubts they threw at him. Before he ever faced Goliath, he first had to overcome the disbelief of those closest to him. His brothers, seasoned soldiers, scoffed at his confidence, dismissing him as an overzealous shepherd unfit for war. Saul, Israel's king, looked at David's youth and inexperience and saw weakness, not potential. Saul and his brothers saw limitations, but David saw purpose.

David refused to let the voices of others define his future or shrink his vision. The world may tell you that you are too small, too inexperienced, or too unqualified, but none of that matters if you refuse to listen.

Success thrives on conviction, not the opinions of others. Those who dare to act, despite doubt, despite obstacles, are the ones who shape their destiny.

David didn't just silence Goliath, he silenced every doubt that had been cast upon him. Success thrives on conviction, not the opinions of others. Those who dare to act, despite doubt, despite obstacles—are the ones who shape their destiny.

Steve Jobs understood the truth many fail to grasp—your identity is not shaped by the circumstances you were born into or the voices that try to diminish your worth. He refused to let his adoption define him, and he rejected the labels others tried to impose. Jobs crushed the doubts that tried to cloud his vision and bulldozed his path to innovation and success. His journey was proof that greatness is not handed down, it is forged by resilience, belief, and the refusal to surrender to the expectations of others.

Life will always present challenges, people will always have opinions, and setbacks will come like waves. However, none of these have the power to dictate your destiny unless you allow them to. Another person's failures do not bind you, nor are you sentenced by the limitations they place on you. God loves you unconditionally and desires your success in every area of life.

One Bible verse powerfully speaks to this truth and is a timeless reminder:

> *"For I know the thoughts that I think toward you, saith the Lord, thoughts of peace, and not of evil, to give you an expected end."*[194]

This promise speaks directly to anyone who feels weighed down by regret or unsure about what's ahead. It's more than comfort, it's a declaration. Your story is not over. The Author of your life has written it with **love, care, and success.**

In The Apple and The Stone, I affirm what both Steve Jobs and David modeled: that purpose can rise from pain. These men didn't wait for ideal conditions, they created value in the middle of uncertainty, and in doing so, redefined what was possible. So can you. Your past doesn't disqualify you; it prepares you.

The question is no longer what have you been through? But what value will you build because of it?

Now go write your future with courage and let the ink of your resilience dry in victory. The pen is in your hands now.

---

194. *KJV*, Jeremiah 29:11.

STRATEGY 12 TAKEAWAYS

Saul and the Men in the Army	Steve Jobs and Teenager David
Failed to create value	Created value for themselves and others
Did not unearth their greatness	Found and used their greatness
Embraced excuses	Obliterated excuses

YOUR TURN TO REFLECT AND ACT

1. How will you create value for yourself and others?

2. What step will you take to uncover and use the greatness within you?

3. How will you delete excuses and relentlessly pursue your goals?

Signature: _____   Today's date: _____

FINAL COMMENTS

David's victory over Goliath and Steve Jobs's transformation of Apple remind us that greatness often rises from unlikely places. The same potential lives in you.

A waken it.

Use it to confront the Goliaths that challenge your purpose and confidence. Be patient with yourself, think boldly, rise when you fall, and keep pursuing the dreams God placed in your heart.

Obstacles are inevitable, but they are not final. Each one hides an opportunity. Hold onto your vision and trust the strength within you.

May God's blessings and guidance be with you always.

Hartford

BIBLIOGRAPHY

Anthony, Scott D. "Kodak's Downfall Wasn't About Technology." *Harvard Business Review*. July 15, 2016. Accessed April 7, 2025. https://hbr.org/2016/07/kodaks-downfall-wasnt-about-technology.

Apple Inc. "Apple Celebrates One Billion iPhones." *Apple Newsroom*. July 27, 2016. https://www.apple.com/newsroom/2016/07/apple-celebrates-one-billion-iphones.

Apple Inc. "Apple Debuts iPhone 16 Pro and iPhone 16 Pro Max." *Apple Newsroom*. September 9, 2024. Accessed June 18, 2025. https://www.apple.com/newsroom/2024/09/apple-debuts-iphone-16-pro-and-iphone-16-pro-max/

Apple Inc. iPad Introduction – Apple Special Event (2010). January 27, 2010. https://www.youtube.com/watch?v=OBhYxj2SvRI.

Apple Inc. "The Spirit of the iPod Lives On." *Apple Newsroom*. May 10, 2022. Accessed June 18, 2025. https://www.apple.com/newsroom/2022/05/the-spirit-of-ipod-lives-on/.

Arslan, Tarik. "The Truth About Michael Jordan Being 'Cut' From His High School Team." *Oldskoolbball*. Accessed June 16, 2025. https://oldskoolbball.com/michael-jordan-high-school-varsity/.

Athavaley, Anjali. "Verizon, Corning Agree to $1.05 Billion Fiber Deal." *Yahoo Finance*. April 4, 2017. https://finance.yahoo.com/news/verizon-corning-agree-1-05-161249110.html.

Bacon, Francis. *The Advancement of Learning*. 1605. Quoted in "The Importance of Logic and Critical Thinking." *Think Reading*. Accessed June 17, 2025. https://thinkreading.commons.gc.cuny.edu/the-importance-of-logic-and-critical-thinking

Bajarin, Tim. "How Apple's iPhone Changed These 5 Major Industries." *Time*. June 26, 2017. Accessed June 20, 2025. https://time.com/4832599/iphone-anniversary-industry-change/.

Bajarin, Tim. "Why Steve Jobs Went 'Thermonuclear' Over Android." PCMag. December 1, 2014. Accessed June 30, 2025. https://www.pcmag.com/opinions/why-steve-jobs-went-thermonuclear-over-android.

Bellis, Mary. "The Failed Inventions of Thomas Alva Edison." *ThoughtCo.* July 3, 2019. https://www.thoughtco.com/thomas-edison-failures-1991687.

Bort, Julie. "Microsoft Invented a Tablet a Decade Before Apple and Totally Blew It." *Business Insider.* May 30, 2013. https://finance.yahoo.com/news/microsoft-invented-tablet-decade-apple-173815913.html.

Bosker, Bianca. "Bill Gates On Steve Jobs In 1998: 'He Knows He Can't Win' (AUDIO)." *HuffPost.* June 12, 2010. https://www.huffpost.com/entry/bill-gates-on-steve-jobs_n_533817.

Boyle, Alan. "3,000-Year-Old Artifacts Reveal History behind Biblical David and Goliath." *NBC News.* May 8, 2012. https://www.nbcnews.com/sciencemain/3-000-year-old-artifacts-reveal-history-behind-biblical-david-761720.

Brennan, Chrisann. *The Bite in the Apple: A Memoir of My Life with Steve Jobs.* New York: St. Martin's Press, 2013.

Bunyan, John. *The Pilgrim's Progress.* London: Printed for Nathaniel Ponder, 1678.

Case Study Inc. "Apple's Four Quadrant Product Grid." *MacWorld Expo.* January 1998. Accessed April 7, 2025. https://www.casestudyinc.com/apples-four-quadrant-product-grid/.

ChristianAnswers.net. . "David's Sling and Stones—Were They Toys or Serious Weapons?" Accessed June 20, 2025. https://christiananswers.net/q-abr/abr-slingsforkids.html.

Collins, Jim. *Good to Great: Why Some Companies Make the Leap.. and Others Don't.* New York: HarperBusiness, 2001.

Corning Incorporated. "Wendell P. Weeks." Accessed April 7, 2025. https://www.corning.com/worldwide/en/about-us/company-profile/our-leadership/wendell-p--weeks.html.

Cuddy, Amy. *Your Body Language May Shape Who You Are.* TED Talk, TEDGlobal 2012. Filmed June 2012. Posted October 2012. Accessed June 20, 2025. https://www.ted.com/talks/amy_cuddy_your_body_language_may_shape_who_you_are.

Dale, David. "How Does a Pilot Remain Calm Under Pressure?" *Avgeekery.* July 7, 2024. Accessed June 20, 2025. https://avgeekery.com/pilots-calm-in-cockpit/.

DaveManuel.com. "Why Did Ronald Wayne Sell His 10% Stake in Apple for Just $800?" *DaveManuel.com.* January 23, 2024. https://www.davemanuel.com/2024/01/23/ronald-wayne-shares-sold-apple/.

Dawson, Victoria. "How Colonel Sanders Made Kentucky Fried Chicken an American Success Story." *Smithsonian Magazine.* July 6, 2015. https://www.smithsonianmag.com/smithsonian-institution/how-colonel-sanders-made-kentucky-fried-chicken-american-success-story-180955806/.\

Diaz, Jesus. "The Inside Story of How the iPad Got Its Iconic Design." *Gizmodo*. November 18, 2013. https://gizmodo.com/the-inside-story-of-how-the-ipad-got -its-iconic-deisgn-1463463557.

Dictionary.com. "Achieve." Accessed April 7, 2025. https://www.dictionary.com/browse/ achieve.

Dormehl, Luke. "Today in Apple History: App Store Opens Its Virtual Doors." *Cult of Mac*. July 10, 2024. Accessed June 20, 2025. https://www.cultofmac.com/news/ apple-app-store-launch.

Elder, Linda. "Why Critical Thinking?" *Foundation for Critical Thinking*. Accessed June 17, 2025. https://www.criticalthinking.org/pages/why-critical-thinking/792.

ESPN News Services. *"CCSU's Aaron Dawson Sets Record with 308 Rushing Yards in a Half."* ESPN. October 28, 2018. https://www.espn.com/college-football/story/_/ id/25101020/ccsu-aaron-dawson-sets-record-308-rushing-yards-half.

Federal Reserve Bank of New York. *Quarterly Report on Household Debt and Credit*. Center for Microeconomic Data. Q4 2024. Accessed June 15, 2025. https://www.newy-orkfed.org/microeconomics/hhdc.html.

Fiore, Neil A. *The Now Habit: A Strategic Program for Overcoming Procrastination and Enjoying Guilt-Free Play*. New York: Penguin Group, 2007.

Fore, Preston. "Apple Cofounder Ronald Wayne Sold His 10% Stake for $800 in 1976— Today It'd Be Worth up to $300 Billion." *Fortune*, June 24, 2025. https://fortune. com/2025/06/24/apple-cofounder-ronald-wayne-sold-10-percent-stake-early-today- worth-300-billion-steve-jobs-steve-wozniak/.

Foundation for Critical Thinking. "About Us." *Foundation for Critical Thinking*. Accessed June 17, 2025. https://www.criticalthinking.org.

Gabriel, Susan. "Kathryn Stockett: *The Help* Turned Down 60 Times." *Susan Gabriel: Southern Novelist*. August 11, 2011. https://www.susangabriel.com/writers-and-writing/ kathryn-stockett

GED Testing Service. *Home – GED*. Accessed June 23, 2025. https://www.ged.com

Goldman, Robert, and Stephen Papson. *Nike Culture: The Sign of the Swoosh*. Thousand Oaks, CA: SAGE Publications, 1998.

Gretzky, Wayne. *99: My Life in Pictures*. Toronto: Mint Publishers, 2000. Quoted in "TOP 25 Quotes by Wayne Gretzky." *A-Z Quotes*. Accessed June 30, 2025. https:// www.azquotes.com/author/5901-Wayne_Gretzky.

Gulacha, Amaan. "The Panama Canal's Role in Strategic Supply Chain Planning." *Forbes*, June 13, 2025. Accessed June 13, 2025. Forbes.

Gustin, Sam. "The Fatal Mistake That Doomed BlackBerry." TIME. September 24, 2013. https://business.time.com/2013/09/24/the-fatal-mistake-that-doomed-blackberry/.

Haden, Jeff. "28 Years Ago, Steve Jobs Overcame This Cognitive Bias to Completely Transform Apple." *Inc.*, May 27, 2025. https://www.inc.com/jeff-haden/28-years-ago-steve-jobs -overcame-this-cognitive-bias-to-completely-transform-apple/91193354

Hayes, Marianne. "Paying Off Debt With the Highest APR vs. Highest Balance." *Experian.* April 19, 2024. https://www.experian.com/blogs/ask-experian/should-i-pay -off-highest-balance-or-highest-interest-first/.

Hill, Napoleon. *Your Big Opportunity May Be Right Where You Are Now.* BrainyQuote. Accessed June 13, 2025. BrainyQuote.

Hobson, Nick. "25 Years Ago, Steve Jobs Saved Apple From Collapse." *Inc.com*, April 19, 2023. Accessed June 12, 2025. Inc.com.

Hoffman, Bobby. "When You Have Too Much Confidence, Expect This to Happen." *Psychology Today.* August 17, 2017. Accessed June 20, 2025. https://www.psychologytoday.com/us/ blog/motivate/201708/when-you-have-too-much-confidence-expect-this-to-happen.

The Holy Bible. King James Version. Oxford: Oxford University Press, 1769.

How KFC's Colonel Sanders Failed 1009 Times." Failure Before Success. April 14, 2020. https://failurebeforesuccess.com/how-kfcs-colonel-sanders-failed-1009-times/.

"How Many Times Did the Wright Brothers Fail?" *Reference.com.* Last modified May 21, 2025. https://www.reference.com/history-geography/many-times-did -wright-brothers-fail-c16b1bcbf2c584e7.

Howes, Lewis. "Lisa Nichols on The Key to Abundance and Success." *The School of Greatness.* Accessed June 16, 2025. https://lewishowes.com/legacy/lisa-nichols/.

Isaacson, Walter. *Steve Jobs.* New York: Simon & Schuster, 2011.

James, Geoffrey. "21 Successful People Who Rebounded After Getting Fired." *Inc.* October 7, 2015. https://www.inc.com/business-insider/21-successful-people-who-rebounded- after-getting-fired.html.

"Jobs Names Apple Board." *CNN Money.* August 6, 1997. Accessed June 20, 2025. https:// money.cnn.com/1997/08/06/technology/apple/.

Jobs, Steve. Interview by Walt Mossberg and Kara Swisher. *D5: All Things Digital Conference.* May 30, 2007. AllThingsD. https://allthingsd.com/20070531/d5-gates -jobs-transcript/.

Jobs, Steve. "iPad Introduction – Apple Special Event (2010)." Apple Inc. January 27, 2010. https://www.youtube.com/watch?v=OBhYxj2SvRI.

Jobs, Steve. "Macworld 2007 Keynote Address." Apple Inc. January 9, 2007. https://www.youtube.com/watch?v=VQKMoT-6XSg.

Jobs, Steve. "My Favorite Things in Life Don't Cost Any Money. It's Really Clear That the Most Precious Resource We All Have Is Time." *BrainyQuote*. Accessed June 20, 2025. https://www.brainyquote.com/quotes/steve_jobs_416854.

Jobs, Steve. "You've Got to Find What You Love, Jobs Says." *Stanford Report*. June 14, 2005. https://news.stanford.edu/stories/2005/06/youve-got-find-love-jobs-says.

Jones, Suzanne W. "The Divided Reception of *The Help*." *JSTOR*, 2009. Accessed June 13, 2025. JSTOR.

Julien's Auctions. "Steve Jobs | Photo-Shoot Worn and Stage-Worn 1984 Macintosh Computer Release Bow Tie (with Book)." *Julien's Auctions*. Accessed June 19, 2025. https://www.juliensauctions.com/en/items/229029/steve-jobs-photo-shoot-worn-and-stage-worn-1984-macintosh-computer-release-bow-tie-with-book.

https://knowledge.wharton.upenn.edu/article/tablet-wars-can-rivals-unseat-the-ipad/.

Khan, Aasma. "Ron Wayne: Apple's Forgotten Founder Who Walked Away." *YourStory*. April 10, 2025. https://yourstory.com/2025/04/ron-wayne-apple-founder-story.

Knowledge at Wharton. "Tablet Wars: Can Rivals Unseat the iPad?" *Wharton School of the University of Pennsylvania*. November 10, 2010.

Kodak. "History | Kodak." *Kodak*. Accessed June 16, 2025. https://www.kodak.com/en/company/page/history/

Lashinsky, Adam. "When Steve Jobs Returned to Apple." Stanford Technology Ventures Program. May 23, 2012. https://stvp.stanford.edu/wp-content/uploads/sites/3/2024/09/when-stevejobs-returned-to-apple-transcript.pdf.

Lobello, Carmel. "The Rise and Fall of Kodak: By the Numbers." *The Week*. January 11, 2015. Accessed April 7, 2025. https://theweek.com/articles/481308/rise-fall-kodak-by-numbers.

Marie, Emma. "What Makes River Stones Shine Smoothly?" *OutdoorMo*. January 19, 2025. https://outdoormo.com/what-makes-river-stones-shine-smoothly.

Markway, Barbara. "Why Self-Confidence Is More Important Than You Think." *Psychology Today*. September 20, 2018. Accessed June 20, 2025. https://www.psychologytoday.com/us/blog/shyness-is-nice/201809/why-self-confidence-is-more-important-you-think.

McInerney, Liam. "World's Fastest Plane Could Have Reached New York from London in 45

McKendrick, Joe. "Steve Jobs: Seven Ways He Taught Us to 'Think Different.'" *ZDNET*.

October 5, 2011. https://www.zdnet.com/article/steve-jobs-seven-ways-he-taught-us-to-think-different/.

Milford Academy, *2016 Football Schedule*, accessed June 16, 2025, https://www.milfordacademy.org/athletics-schedule-2016.html.

Media Shower. "How Steve Jobs's 'Think Different' Speech Saved Apple." *Media Shower.* July 22, 2024. https://mediashower.com/blog/steve-jobs-1997-speech/.

Merriam-Webster. *Obstacle.* Accessed June 26, 2025. https://www.merriam-webster.com/dictionary/obstacle.

Merriam-Webster. *Opportunity.* Accessed June 26, 2025. https://www.merriam-webster.com/dictionary/opportunity.

Merriam-Webster. *Passion. Merriam-Webster.com Dictionary.* Accessed April 7, 2025. https://www.merriam-webster.com/dictionary/passion.

Milton, John. *Paradise Lost.* London: Samuel Simmons, 1667.

Minutes." *Express.* February 8, 2025. Accessed June 20, 2025. https://www.express.co.uk/news/world/2011012/worlds-fastest-plane-4520mph.

Mother Teresa. *Mother Teresa's Golden Words.* Mother Teresa Charitable Trust. Accessed June 30, 2025. https://www.motherteresacharities.org/mother-teresa-Quotes.php.

NASA Glenn Research Center. "Guide to Aerodynamics." *Beginners Guide to Aeronautics.* Accessed June 18, 2025. https://www1.grc.nasa.gov/beginners-guide-to-aeronautics/learn-about-aerodynamics/.

Nichols, Lisa. "The Secret to More Happiness, Success, & Wellness." *The Model Health Show.* Hosted by Shawn Stevenson. Episode 773. Accessed June 15, 2025. https://themodelhealthshow.com/happiness-success-wellness/.

"9 Benefits of Playing Chess." *Healthline.* Accessed June 17, 2025. https://www.healthline.com/health/benefits-of-playing-chess.

Olson, Parmy. "BlackBerry's Famous Last Words At 2007 iPhone Launch: 'We'll Be Fine.'" *Forbes.* May 26, 2015. https://www.forbes.com/sites/parmyolson/2015/05/26/blackberry-iphone-book.

Peale, Norman Vincent. *The Power of Positive Thinking.* Englewood Cliffs, NJ: Prentice Hall, 1952.

Persson, Emil. "Apple: From Garage Upstart to Global Giant." *Quartr.* June 19, 2024. https://quartr.com/insights/company-research/apple-from-garage-upstart-to-global-giant.

Planes, Alex. "The Day Apple and Microsoft Traded Places." *The Motley Fool.* August 6,

2013. Accessed June 30, 2025. https://www.fool.com/investing/general/2013/08/06/the-day-apple-and-microsoft-traded-places.aspx

Powers, Jeffrey. *September 12, 1985: Steve Jobs Leaves Apple to Start NeXT.* Day in Tech History, September 12, 2018. Accessed June 12, 2025. https://dayintechhistory.com/dith/september-12-1985-steve-jobs-leaves-apple-start-2/.

Preville, Philip. *The Professor's Guide to Using Bloom's Taxonomy.* Chicago: Loyola University Chicago, 2023. https://www.luc.edu/media/lucedu/clas/Bloom's%20Taxonomy_2023.pdf.

Pryce, Nikkie. *Dreamers, Take Action.* Opportune Independent Publishing Company, 2017.

Reading Rockets. *Bloom's Taxonomy Questions.* Accessed June 17, 2025. https://www.readingrockets.org/sites/default/files/2023-09/Blooms%20Taxonomy%20questions.pdf.

Rowe, Patrick. "Michael Jordan Quit Basketball to Play a Completely Different Sport During the Peak of His Career." *SPORTbible.* April 9, 2023. https://www.sportbible.com/nba/michael-jordan-baseball-career-analysed-chicago-bulls-114256-20230409.

Ruhl, Charlotte. "Bloom's Taxonomy of Learning." *Simply Psychology.* Last updated March 11, 2025. Accessed June 17, 2025. https://www.simplypsychology.org/blooms-taxonomy.html.

Ryu, Soomin, and Lu Fan. "The Relationship Between Financial Worries and Psychological Distress Among U.S. Adults." *Journal of Family and Economic Issues* 44 (2023): 16–33. Accessed June 17, 2025. https://link.springer.com/article/10.1007/s10834-022-09820-9.

Sahu, Aparna. "Michael Dell's Journey: From Dorm Room to Tech Titan." *The Entrepreneur Story.* June 25, 2024. https://theentrepreneurstory.com/business/michael-dells-journey-from-dorm-room-to-tech-titan/.

Schlender, Brent, and Rick Tetzeli. *Becoming Steve Jobs: The Evolution of a Reckless Upstart into a Visionary Leader.* New York: Crown Business, 2015.

Scott, Stuart. "When You Die, It Does Not Mean That You Lose to Cancer." *V Foundation.* January 4, 2015. Accessed April 7, 2025. https://www.v.org/story/when-you-die-it-does-not-mean-that-you-lose-to-cancer-stuart-scott/.

Seiter, Tasha. "Love and Money: How Financial Stress Affects Relationships." *Psychology Today.* April 20, 2025. Accessed June 17, 2025. https://www.psychologytoday.com/us/blog/mindful-relationships/202503/love-and-money-how-financial-stress-affects-relationships

Seth, Shobhit. "BlackBerry: A Story of Constant Success and Failure." Investopedia. Last updated March 7, 2025. https://www.investopedia.com/articles/investing/062315/blackberry-story-constant-success-failure.asp.

Silver, Stephen. "August 6, 1997—The Day Apple and Microsoft Made Peace." *AppleInsider*, August 6, 2018. https://appleinsider.com/articles/18/08/06/august-6-1997----the-day-apple-and-microsoft-made-peace.

Smith, Jeff. "Corning Inc. Building New $900 Million Solar Facility in Michigan Updates." *The Leader*. February 14, 2025. Accessed April 7, 2025. https://www.the-leader.com/story/news/local/2025/02/14/corning-inc-building-new-900-million-solar-facility-in-michigan-updates/78454504007/

Stockett, Kathryn. *The Help* (Amy Einhorn Books/Putnam, 2009)

Suarez, Jacob. "How Steve Jobs's 1997 Return to Apple Saved the Company." *SlashGear*, April 19, 2022. Accessed June 13, 2025. SlashGear.

The Terminator. Directed by James Cameron. Los Angeles: Orion Pictures, 1984.

"Top 10 Tech Companies by Market Cap 2025." *Financial Express*. May 3, 2025. https://www.financialexpress.com/trending/top-10-tech-companies-by-market-cap-2025-who-leads-globally-and-where-does-india-stand/3831051/.

United States Marine Corps. "Recruit Training." Accessed April 7, 2025. https://www.marines.com/become-a-marine/process-to-join/recruit-training.html.

University of Cambridge. "The Rise and Fall of Kodak's Moment." *University of Cambridge*. February 27, 2012. https://www.cam.ac.uk/research/news/the-rise-and-fall-of-kodaks-moment.

Verganti, Roberto. "Apple's Secret? It Tells Us What We Should Love." *Harvard Business Review*. January 28, 2010. https://hbr.org/2010/01/how-apple-innovates-by-telling.

Walker, Caroline. "Classic Video of Steve Jobs Wearing Shorts While Presenting His New Vision for Apple." *MethodShop*. September 26, 2023. https://methodshop.com/steve-jobs-wearing-shorts/

Ward, Marguerite. "7 Body-Language Tricks to Exude Confidence." *CNBC*. September 14, 2016. Accessed June 20, 2025. https://www.cnbc.com/2016/09/14/7-body-language-tricks-to-exude-confidence.html.

Wayne, Ronald G. "Why I Left Apple Computer After Only 12 Days." Facebook post, February 22, 2012. Quoted in *Mac History*, February 23, 2012. https://www.mac-history.net/2012/02/23/ron-wayne-why-i-left-apple-computer-after-only-12-days/.

Why Did David Pick Up Five Stones When He Faced Goliath (1 Sam. 17:40)?" *BibleQ.net*. Accessed June 17, 2025. https://bibleq.net/answer/2820.

Winfrey, Oprah, and Janet Lowe. *Oprah Winfrey Speaks: Insight from the World's Most Influential Voice*. New York: John Wiley & Sons, 1998.

Winkelman, Steven. "Leaked Internal Memo Warns Apple Employees About Dangers of Leaking." *Digital Trends*. April 13, 2018. Accessed April 7, 2025. https://www.digitaltrends.com/mobile/apple-leak-letter-2018/.

Yahoo Finance. "Apple Inc. (AAPL) Stock Historical Prices & Data." *Yahoo Finance*. Accessed June 30, 2025. https://finance.yahoo.com/quote/AAPL/history.

Yahoo Finance. "Corning Inc (GLW) Q4 2024 Earnings Call Highlights." *Yahoo Finance*. February 1, 2025. Accessed April 7, 2025. https://finance.yahoo.com/news/corning-inc-glw-q4-2024-071547483.html.

QUOTE SOURCES

Strategy 1: Steve Jobs: Steve Jobs, Stanford Commencement Address, June 12, 2005. Stanford University.

Strategy 2: David: *Psalm 18:34*, King James Version. *The Holy Bible, King James Version*. Cambridge: Cambridge University Press, 1769.

Strategy 3: Steve Jobs: Steve Jobs, Stanford Commencement Address, June 12, 2005. Stanford University.

Strategy 4: David: *Psalm 18:29*, King James Version. *The Holy Bible, King James Version*. Cambridge: Cambridge University Press, 1769.

Strategy 5: Steve Jobs: "Here's to the Crazy Ones," Apple Inc. commercial, 1997. Quoted in ZDNet.

Strategy 6: David: *2 Samuel 22:40*, King James Version. *The Holy Bible, King James Version*. Cambridge: Cambridge University Press, 1769.

Strategy 7: Steve Jobs: Steve Jobs, interview with Daniel Morrow, *Smithsonian Oral History Project*, April 20, 1995. Quoted in Inc.

Strategy 8: David: *1 Samuel 17:46*, King James Version. *The Holy Bible, King James Version*. Cambridge: Cambridge University Press, 1769.

Strategy 9: Steve Jobs: Steve Jobs, Stanford Commencement Address, June 12, 2005. Stanford University.

Strategy 10: David: *Psalm 23:4*, King James Version. *The Holy Bible, King James Version*. Cambridge: Cambridge University Press, 1769.

Strategy 11: Steve Jobs: Steve Jobs, quoted in *The Steve Jobs Way* by Jay Elliot (New York: Vanguard Press, 2011), 125.

Strategy 12: Steve Jobs: Steve Jobs, quoted in *Steve Jobs: The Exclusive Biography* by Walter Isaacson (New York: Simon & Schuster, 2011), 567.

ABOUT THE AUTHOR

Hartford G. Dawson, PhD, is a Jamaican-born writer and U.S.-educated professor whose work bridges inspiration with impact. He holds a doctorate in Information Technology, specializing in IT Education, from Capella University, and lives in New York with his wife and three sons.

With over thirty years of experience in the IT industry and teaching roles at both secular and Christian universities, Hartford blends technical depth with spiritual insight. His work is known for its emotional resonance, strategic clarity, and motivational force. As a conference speaker and podcast guest, he brings these qualities to the page, the podium, and the microphone, sharing insights on resilience, leadership, motivation, and purpose.

After a life-threatening illness linked to his 2014 visit to Africa, Hartford founded Love Without Walls, a nonprofit building a children's hospital in Suhum, Ghana—set to open in 2026. Learn more at LoveWithoutWalls.org. Through his writing, he empowers readers to face life's giants with courage, purpose, and momentum, helping them uncover the strength in their struggles and the victories hidden in plain sight.

To connect with Hartford or explore his work further, visit

HARTFORDDAWSON.COM

You have taken a powerful step by reading *The Apple and The Stone*.

The Apple and The Stone Workbook is designed to help you apply all twelve strategies to your own life with clarity, confidence, and purpose. Inside, you will find guided questions, action steps, reflection prompts, and space to work through the giants you are facing.

Access it here: **www.HartfordDawson.com/printworkbook**

Or scan the QR code below:

PREFER TO TYPE YOUR ANSWERS OR WORK DIGITALLY?

You can type directly into the reflection questions, action plans, and journaling sections.

Access it here: **www.HartfordDawson.com/workbook**

Or scan the QR code below:

The digital edition is secure, password-protected, and personalized for your use.

THANK YOU FOR READING

If this book encouraged or challenged you, I would be grateful if you left a quick review. Your feedback helps more readers discover *The Apple and The Stone.*

Scan the QR code to leave a review on Amazon.

Thank you for your support!
Hartford

Ready to activate the 12 life-changing strategies from The Apple and The Stone *in real time?* **The Breaking Goliaths App** is your AI-powered companion—built to help you overcome fear, doubt, and resistance with the boldness of David and the creative drive of Steve Jobs. This step-by-step digital coach helps you set goals, break barriers, and build lasting momentum.

Scan below to begin your journey, or visit

HARTFORDDAWSON.COM